An Introduction to Digital Tools for Theatre Designers

Technical drawing.

CGI rendering.

Scale model.

Finished set on stage.

An Introduction to Digital Tools for Theatre Designers

Colin Winslow

THE CROWOOD PRESS

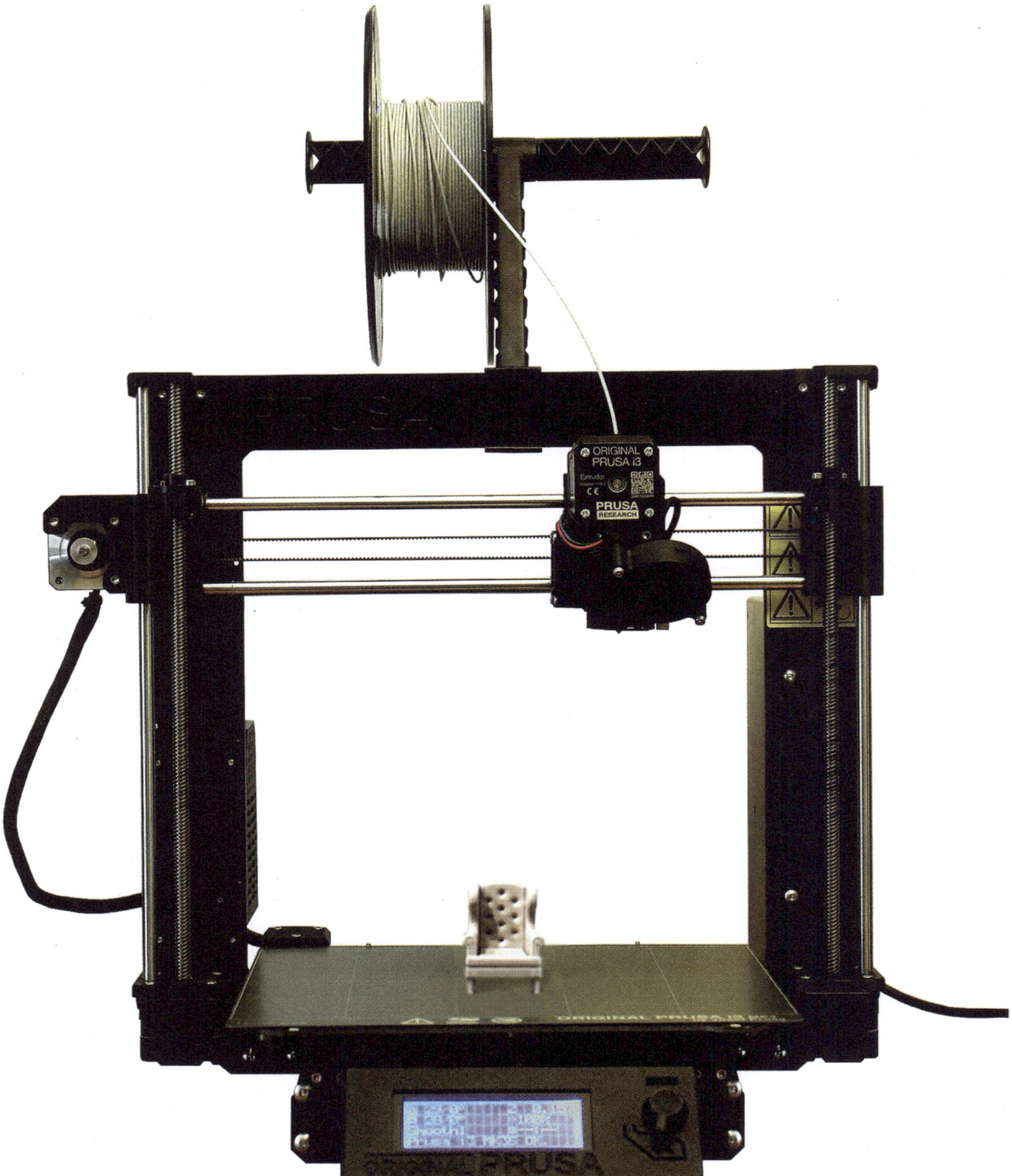
ORIGINAL
PRUSA i3
PRUSA
RESEARCH
PRUSA

CONTENTS

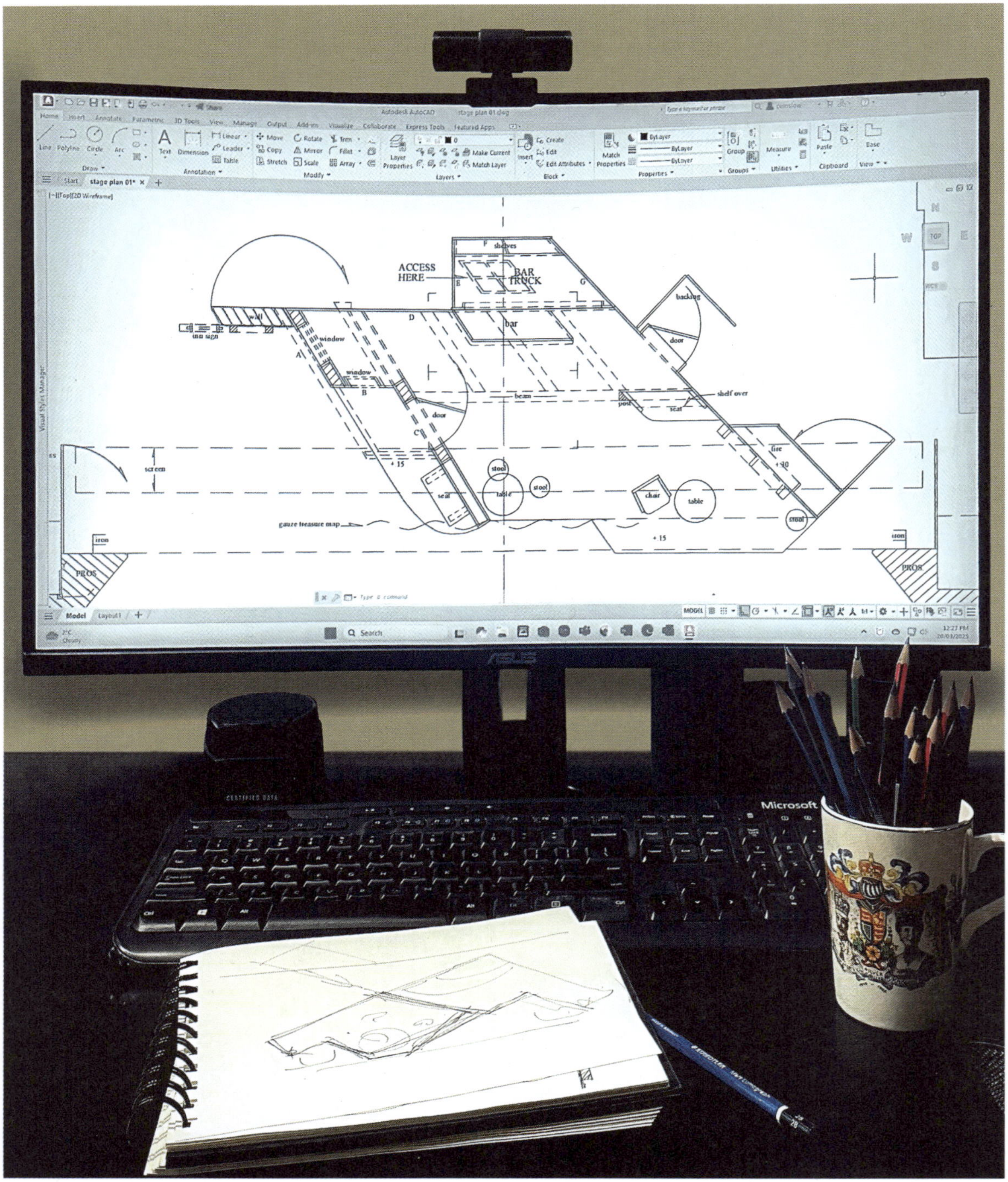
Autodesk AutoCAD
stage plan 01.dwg
shelves
ACCESS HERE
BAR TRUCK
backing
wall
inn sign
bar
door
window
beam
shelf over
post
seat
fire
screen
stool
table
chair
gauze treasure map
iron
PROS
+ 15
Microsoft

INTRODUCTION

This book is not aimed at computer geeks, but at theatre designers who want to explore ways in which some of the most helpful digital techniques may be integrated into their work. Most of us use computers for messaging and word-processing, and we probably enhance our photographs with some basic graphics software, but in the day-to-day use of our computers we do not encounter those more specialised processes such as CAD, CGI and 3D modelling, which are of particular interest to stage designers. These are complex programs, and having installed them on our computers, we need to work through the downloaded instruction manuals and tutorials to learn how to use all the various functions that the software can perform. Unfortunately, the manuals do not tell us which are the most useful features for our work in theatre design, nor how we may best apply them. This we have to discover for ourselves by trial and error. The aim of this book is to remove some of that 'error'.

THE THEATRE DESIGNER'S TASK

Theatre, at its most basic, is a means of communication, whether through speech, song, dance or mime. Sometimes it may tell a story intended simply to entertain and amuse, and at other times it may stir up deep emotions or promote revolutionary ideas – but whatever kind of theatre it may be, the designer's task is to help the performers to communicate with their audiences by creating a space in which a specific presentation can most effectively take place.

The celebrated American stage designer, Oliver Smith, said '… I think the purpose of the designer is to service the director and playwright and the composer, and not to show off …'. This is self-evidently true, but in spite of this, there are times when the creation of spectacular stage imagery or special effects does become part of the designer's job – in shows such as *The Phantom of the Opera*, or the 'transformation scene' in a traditional pantomime, for example. Here the designer is required to be both a creative artist and a practical stage technician, qualities that are frequently found to be in conflict with each other.

So theatre designers are presented with a double task: part conceptual and part technical. It is on the conceptual side that our computers are least helpful, for even with the aid of Artificial Intelligence, they cannot create a truly original idea – to do this, some input from human artistic inspiration and creativity is required. By providing access to the internet, computers can certainly become an invaluable tool for research, but that is not particularly helpful until the designer has at least a tentative notion of a design concept in mind – and even then, the resources of a good library should not be overlooked. However, at the stage when the conceptual aspect is being developed into practicality, a computer becomes virtually essential.

Theatre designers work within severe restraints, for in addition to forming part of a creative concept,

AutoCAD work screen and pencil-sketch plan for a scene in *Treasure Island* at Theatr Clwyd.

whatever we place on stage must be practical: scenery must conform to the theatre's safety regulations, for instance, but it should not impede the performers – and if any scenic transitions are to take place, they must be capable of smooth and efficient operation; costumes must be appropriate for the characters portrayed, but must also permit whatever freedom of movement may be required. Then, having developed a design scheme and coped with the technicalities, the designer must be able to communicate it, with detailed precision, to the director, performers, set builders, scene painters, costume makers, stage technicians and any other designers involved in the production.

A wide range of technical skills is therefore required to produce all those plans, working drawings, costume renderings and detailed scale models, which are never seen by the audience but are of major importance for the practical realisation of the designer's work. Huge advantages are offered here by supplementing the designer's traditional skills with computerised technology – not least the advantage of increased speed, for in the world of theatre, the ability to meet prescribed deadlines is absolutely essential: the first performance before an audience will take place at a specific time on a specific day, and for this to happen, designs *must* be available when they have been scheduled or the result will be increased costs, skimped construction, and a probable lack of future employment for the designer concerned.

DON'T THROW AWAY YOUR PENCILS

It should not be forgotten that the most significant technical advance for theatre designers occurred long before the advent of computers: it was way back in the mid-sixteenth century, and was the result of the accidental discovery of a lavish seam of graphite in the north of England. For artists and designers it was an event that had such far-reaching consequences that it changed the way they worked forever. Before that time, tools for drawing consisted of pen and ink, charcoal, chalk and silver-point – none of which has the versatility or convenience of a graphite pencil, which, although small enough to slip into a pocket, is capable of producing an infinite range of linear and textural qualities simply by varying its angle and the pressure of the fingers. With later improvements by M. Conté in France, this near-perfect drawing instrument is still in daily use and remarkably inexpensive – especially when compared to the price of a computer and graphics software.

Sadly, pencils are now so commonplace that they rarely receive the appreciation they deserve, but even in this digital age, every designer's workspace will inevitably have at least one pencil within easy reach, for a pencil is still the best tool for rapid visualisation of ideas. There are times, especially at the earliest stages in the development of a design scheme, or during creative discussions with the director, when the designer will automatically reach for pencil and paper, because a computer, with its more cumbersome physical structure and its emphasis on precision, is less helpful at this very important stage.

However, when the designer's initial ideas have been developed a little further, a different kind of imagery is needed, because those initial concepts now have to be refined and adapted to suit a specific performance space, and it is when converting those rough pencil sketches into accurate working drawings that digital techniques really come into their own. Software such as *AutoCAD* is designed to perform just this kind of task, and with its help a designer can produce technical drawings of greater accuracy and higher quality, and much faster than is possible with a pencil or draughting pen. Moreover, with the application of more sophisticated techniques, fully coloured three-dimensional digital models, complete with appropriate textures and lighting effects, can be developed from the two-dimensional drawings to give an accurate, detailed impression of how the finished design will appear to an audience.

A costume designer is usually expected to produce a design on paper for each costume, including accessories such as footwear, wigs and jewellery, to give a reasonably good impression of how the finished costume will look when worn on stage – and frequently some explanatory notes and detail sketches will be included on the same sheet. This is where a pencil and some freehand drawing skills with added colour are most helpful. It is quite possible to produce an entire set of costume drawings on a computer (*see* Chapter 7), but in contrast to the technical drawings needed for scenery construction, these can take longer to produce and are far less versatile than the traditional methods. A stylus and graphics tablet, which gives much the same feeling as drawing with a pencil on paper, is a frequent substitute for a computer's mouse when drawing with bitmapped graphics software such as *Photoshop* – but it cannot teach you how to draw, so designers will always need to acquire at least some basic drawing skills by other means.

TRADITIONAL VERSUS DIGITAL SKILLS

It is difficult to imagine life without computers. Not only do we use them continuously in our personal lives for communication, information, shopping and entertainment, but in most professions, including theatre design, they are literally indispensable. However, for theatre designers, such a huge range of digital techniques is now available that to decide which of them can be most useful to us in our work and the best ways to exploit them requires some careful consideration. Sheer delight in the technology can easily lead us astray, and very elegant, digitally produced sheets of technical drawings, or elaborate models from a 3D printer, do not necessarily result in a higher quality of design when the work is eventually realised on stage. A designer's artistic creativity cannot be replaced by a computer, and even in some of the more mundane tasks, there are times when traditional methods still hold an advantage. It is only when the newer digital techniques are used in combination with the older traditional skills that they become a really powerful aid to the theatre designer in developing and communicating creative ideas.

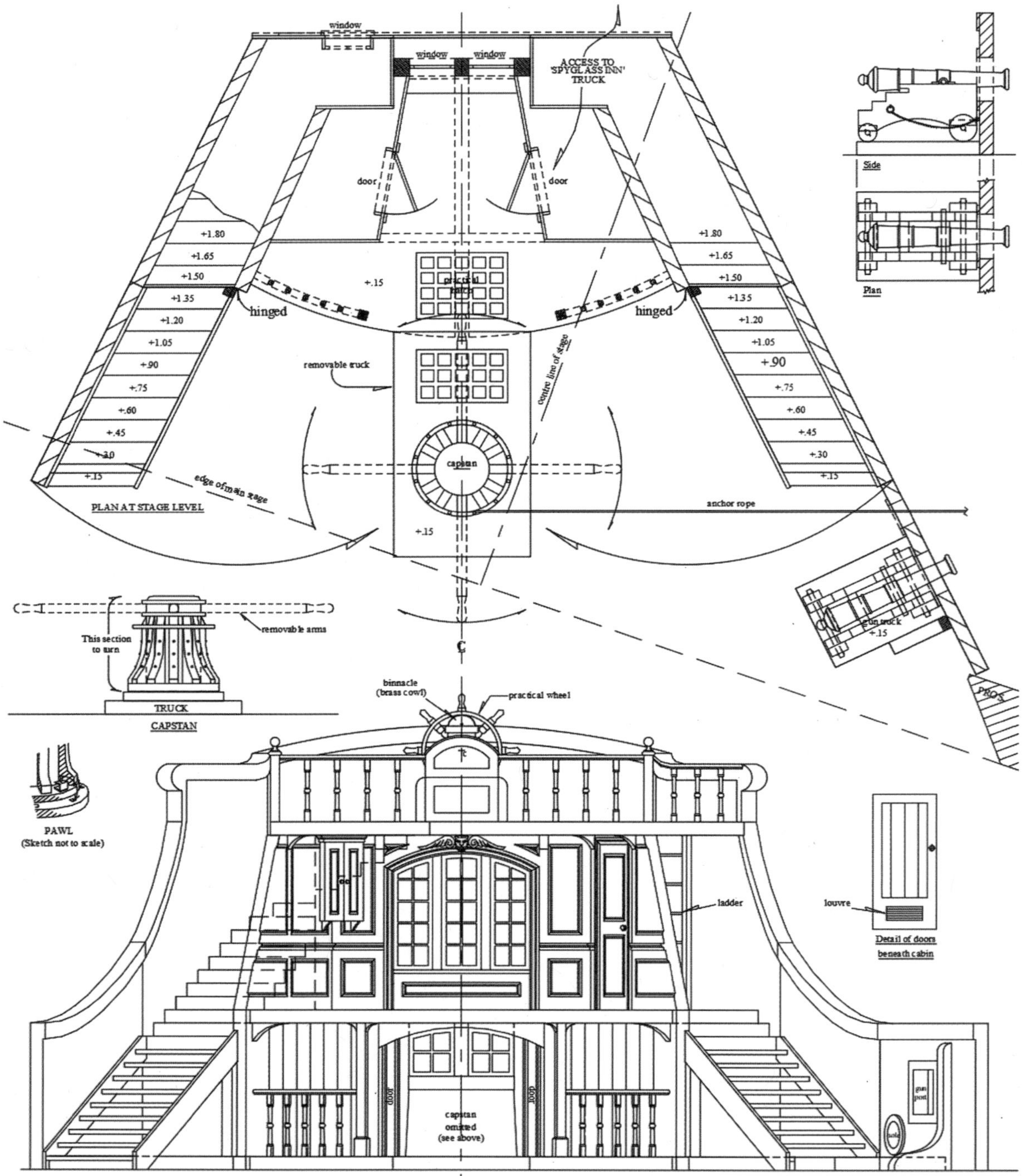

window
window
window
ACCESS TO 'SPYGLASS INN' TRUCK
door
door
+1.80
+1.65
+1.50
+1.35
+1.20
+1.05
+.90
+.75
+.60
+.45
+.30
+.15
+.15
practical hatch
hinged
hinged
removable truck
centre line of stage
capstan
edge of main stage
PLAN AT STAGE LEVEL
anchor rope
+.15
Side
Plan
gun truck
+.15
PROS
removable arms
This section to turn
TRUCK
CAPSTAN
binnacle (brass cowl)
practical wheel
PAWL
(Sketch not to scale)
ladder
louvre
Detail of doors beneath cabin
door
door
capstan omitted (see above)
gun port

1
COMPUTER-AIDED DESIGN

Before the advent of computer-aided design (CAD) a large part of the set designer's working hours was spent in producing stage plans and technical drawings by hand, usually at A1 or A0 sizes. This necessitated the use of a drawing board – a sizeable piece of equipment that took up a large part of the designer's work space. The drawing board was usually equipped with a parallel rule and set squares, or with a (notoriously inaccurate) 'draughting machine'.

A hard, sharp-pointed pencil was used for the initial drawings, but to produce really good prints, the final version had to be drawn in ink on tracing paper or plastic film, using draughting pens of an appropriate size for the thickness of line required. It was virtually impossible to correct errors, and a mere slip of the pen often meant restarting the whole process. Most designers became reasonably proficient in hand-draughting, but the final and most time-consuming part of the whole process was adding the dimension lines, captions and text. If the designer was not blessed with a good freehand lettering ability, this had to be done with the aid of lettering stencils and a pen of compatible size, and could easily take up a whole working day.

Eventually the completed tracing would be taken to a copy bureau where the required number of copies were printed on to special paper by the light-sensitive 'dyeline' process. This was an accurate and fairly inexpensive method of reproduction,

A drawing board, essential for hand-draughting.

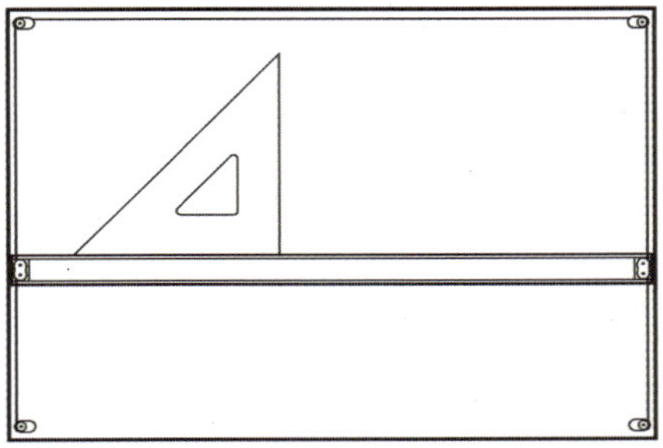

Parallel rule and set square for accurate horizontal and vertical lines.

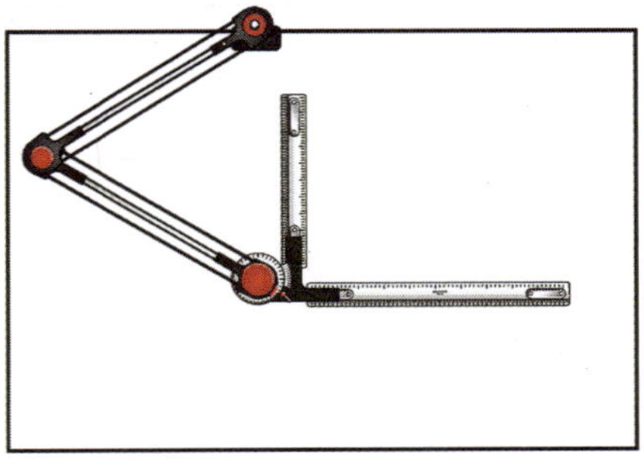

A draughting machine – more sophisticated than a parallel rule, but usually less accurate.

Technical drawings for *Treasure Island* at Theatr Clwyd created in *AutoCAD.*

Lettering stencil for use with a draughting pen of compatible size.

but the prints faded over time, and the chemicals involved produced foul-smelling ammonia fumes that closely resembled the smell of cats' urine and frequently caused embarrassment when carrying a roll of freshly printed dyelines on public transport.

CAD eliminated most of these problems: it takes up very little space in the studio; it is much faster than draughting by hand; and the addition of dimension lines and text, in a font of whatever style and size is preferred, is usually the quickest part of the entire process. The need for hard copies still usually requires a trip to a copy bureau, but dyeline printers became obsolete in the 1980s, and were replaced by large-format ink-jet printer/plotters that can produce prints in full colour at whatever scale is required, and are completely odourless!

The first CAD programs were developed in the early 1960s, but as they had to be run on specialised mainframe computers, they were not generally available to users such as theatre designers. However, by 1980 children were learning how to use computers at school, and the 'home computer' had arrived, usually with some built-in graphics capabilities. In 1982 the Commodore 64 was introduced, which soon became a runaway best-seller for anyone interested in design. It was reasonably priced, and had, for its time, very advanced colour graphics with sixty-four available colours: hence the name.

The *Commodore 64* – a home computer with innovative graphical capabilities.

The *Amiga 1000* – also from Commodore, with even more sophisticated graphics.

In 1985 the Amiga (also from Commodore) supplanted the Commodore 64 – an even more sophisticated computer with wonderful state-of-the-art graphics and 256 colours! (Why would anyone ever need more?) This computer was involved in the creation of some of the amazingly realistic dinosaurs in the first *Jurassic Park* film, but unfortunately the company went bankrupt in

1994, mainly due to poor marketing and the fact that files could be saved only in its own specific non-transferable formats.

By this time most designers had a PC or a Mac in their studio, and in 1982 the first *AutoCAD* software package was released. It was originally designed to run on a PC, and although 'conversion' programs were quickly developed they had varying degrees of success. A dedicated Mac version finally became available in 1992, but in spite of this, many users still find that it runs a little more smoothly on the Windows operating system.

AUTOCAD

AutoCAD (https://www.autodesk.com/products/autocad) is by far the most popular professional CAD system for architects, engineers and interior designers worldwide, and is recognised as the industry-standard software for theatre designers – although many other CAD packages are also in use. In its early days, many users interpreted 'CAD' to mean 'computer-aided drawing' rather than 'computer-aided design', but *AutoCAD*, and most other CAD programs, is capable of a great many more functions than just drawing. These include the creation of photo-realistic renderings of three-dimensional environments, walk-through videos, and 'solid' digital objects that can be exported to a format suitable for 3D printing, and they usually come with an impressive library of adaptable materials and textures for use in the creation of realistic digital imagery.

These advanced features may take some time and effort to master, but with their help, detailed full-colour renderings of complete stage sets can be produced that are far more accurate and convincing than images created by hand. Most of the examples of CGI (computer-generated imagery) in this book were created with *AutoCAD.*

AutoCAD can be expensive. It is available from Autodesk Inc. by annual or monthly subscription, with a 30-day free trial. The annual subscription, which offers a 33 per cent discount over a monthly one, is the more popular. However, as with all Autodesk products, if you are a student, or otherwise involved in education, you can access a free educational version with a twelve-month renewable licence.

To obtain it, go to the 'Autodesk Education Community' page on the Autodesk website, and create an account. You will need to verify your educational status by providing some appropriate documentation such as a student ID, but once accepted, you can download any of the wide range of Autodesk products, including an '*AutoCAD* for Mac' version. The free version has all the same 3D and rendering functions as the fully priced version, the only noticeable difference being that, as it is not intended for commercial use, when you print out your drawings to hard copy, the words 'Educational Version' will appear in the margins on all four sides.

An *AutoCAD LT* version is also available, which is considerably cheaper; however, it lacks most of the advanced functions that are particularly useful to theatre designers, and cannot be used for anything other than 2D draughting.

CAD DRAUGHTING STANDARDS

The Association of British Theatre Technicians (ABTT), in association with the International Organisation of Scenographers, Theatre Architects and Technicians (OISTAT), has established a set of recommended CAD standard formats for use when draughting for the theatre. They can be found on the website of David Ripley (https://cad4theatre.org.uk), who has been involved in providing *AutoCAD* training for the theatre for a great many years, and was instrumental in establishing these standards. His site also contains a blank set-up file designed specifically for theatre work that contains suggested layers, line weights, styles and so on, intended for use with all CAD software, not just *AutoCAD*. Links to the USA (USITT) and Canadian (CITT) draughting standards are also included.

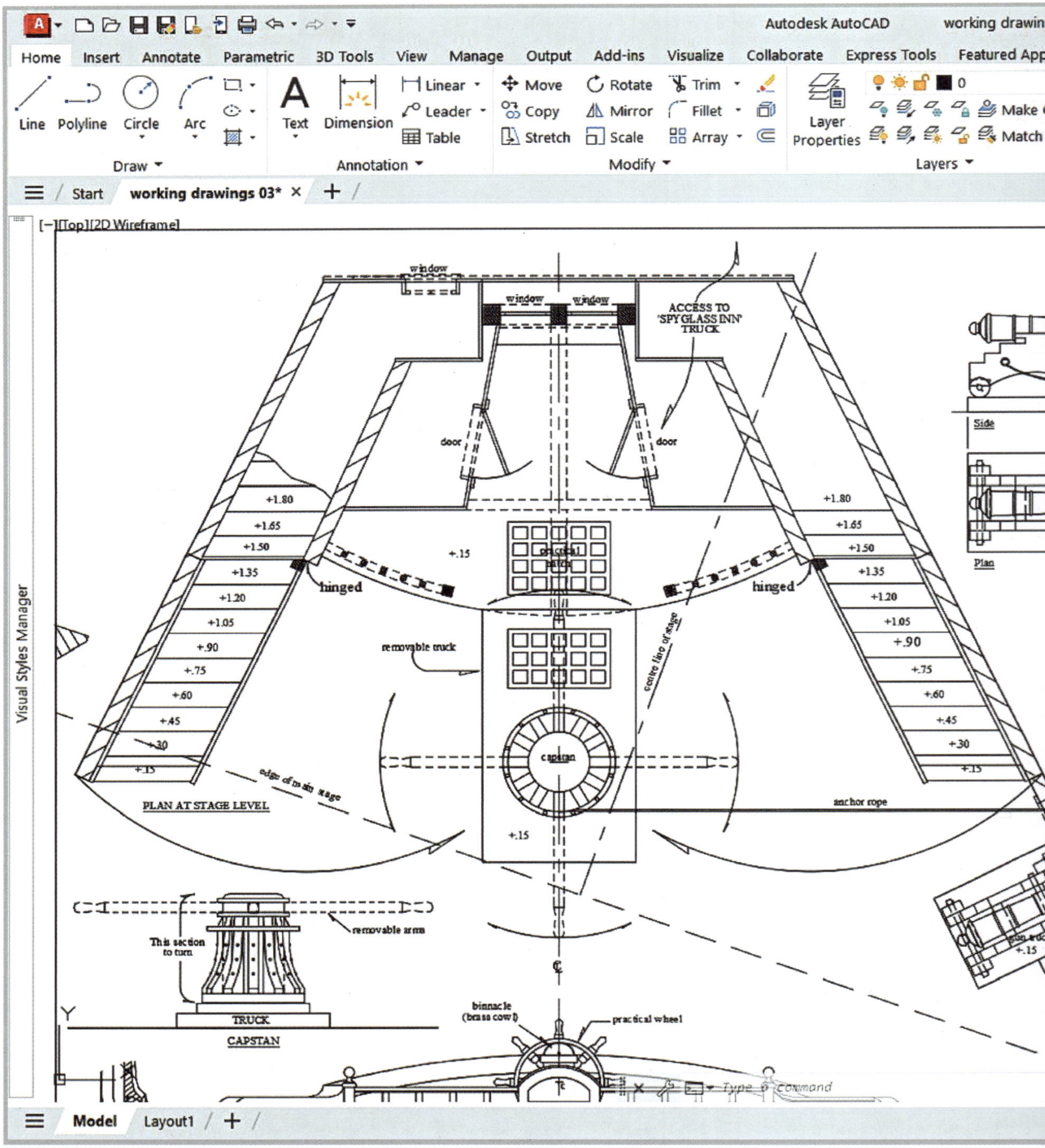

The *AutoCAD* work screen.

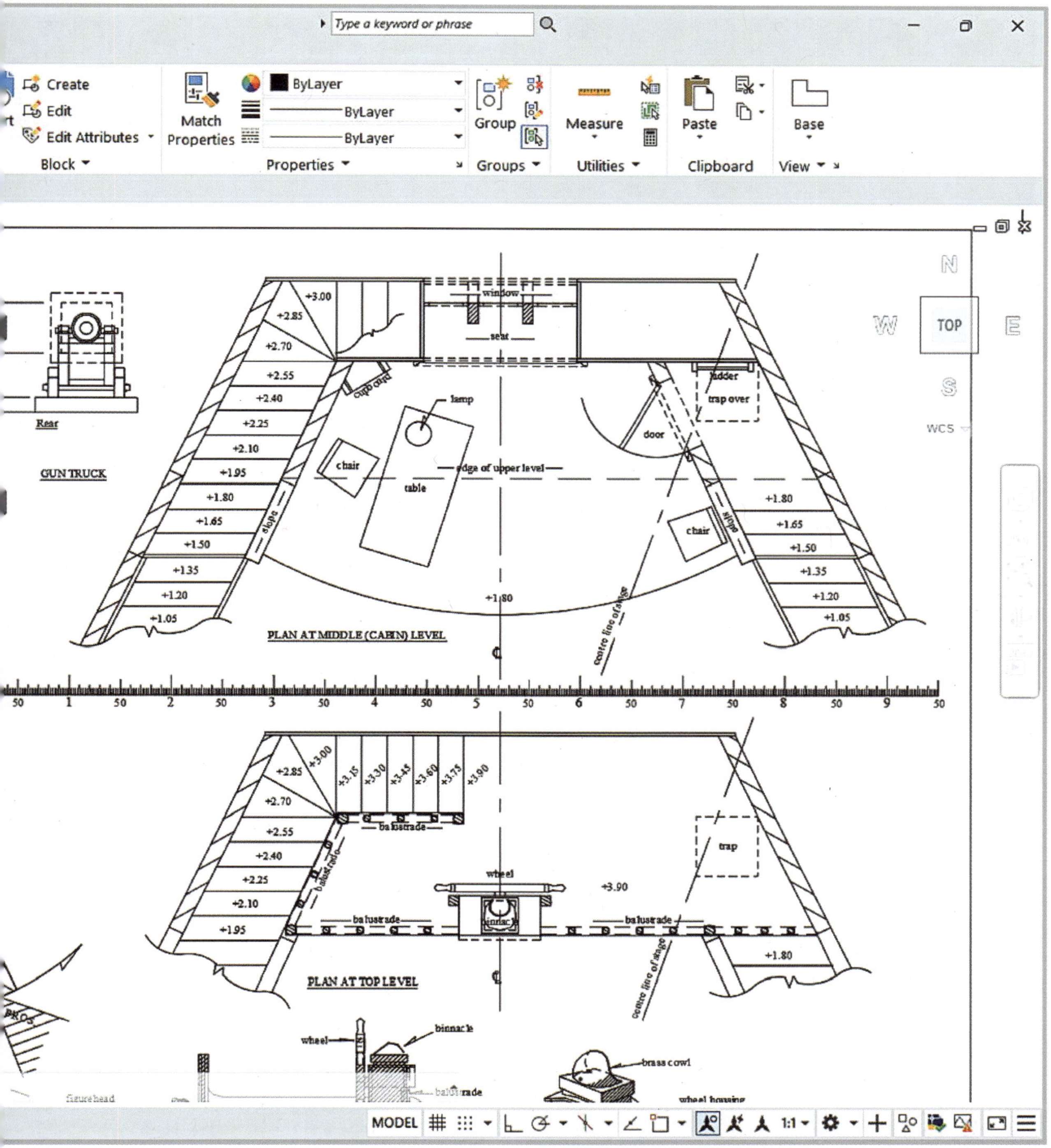
Type a keyword or phrase
Create
Edit
Edit Attributes
Block
Match Properties
ByLayer
ByLayer
ByLayer
Properties
Group
Groups
Measure
Utilities
Paste
Clipboard
Base
View
N
W
TOP
E
S
WCS
Rear
GUN TRUCK
window
seat
cupboard
lamp
ladder
trap over
door
chair
table
edge of upper level
slope
+3.00
+2.85
+2.70
+2.55
+2.40
+2.25
+2.10
+1.95
+1.80
+1.65
+1.50
+1.35
+1.20
+1.05
+1.80
PLAN AT MIDDLE (CABIN) LEVEL
centre line of stage
+3.15
+3.30
+3.45
+3.60
+3.75
+3.90
balustrade
trap
wheel
binnacle
PLAN AT TOP LEVEL
binnacle
balustrade
brass cowl
figurehead
wheel housing
MODEL
1:1

Four Underused *AutoCAD* Commands

PURGE: One of the most helpful *AutoCAD* functions is its ability to revert to an earlier state by stepping back through a lengthy sequence of previous actions. This can be a life saver, but it means that a great many previous versions of the drawing are retained in the program's memory, creating a very large file that can sometimes cause problems and slow down or disable some of the functions. This problem can be eliminated with the 'PURGE' command: select the 'PURGE ALL' option, and you are offered a list of any layers, blocks or line types that are not currently in use, and any that are no longer needed can be permanently eradicated. *AutoCAD* is memory hungry, so it's a good idea to do this at the end of any lengthy work session.

BREP: Short for 'boundary representation'. It is used to reduce file size by removing the entire 'history' from a 3D object and retaining only its basic shape and dimensions. This is particularly useful before saving the final version of an elaborate model, or when exporting a complex object to STL format for 3D printing.

FLATTEN: Sometimes what appears to be a two-dimensional image when viewed from the top, actually contains some lines that have been accidentally created running at an angle in or out of the picture plane instead of in line with it. Use of this command instantly snaps all lines into the same flat plane.

OVERKILL: Occasionally two or more lines can be accidentally created exactly on top of each other giving them the appearance of a single line, which can sometimes cause perplexing problems if this is not recognised. This command will convert them to a single line.

OTHER POPULAR CAD PACKAGES

Listed below are some popular alternatives to *AutoCAD* with varying degrees of complexity and ease of use. When selecting a CAD package, bear in mind that the most common file format industry-wide is DWG, which, although it is actually an abbreviation for 'drawing', is also used for files in 3D formats. Always check that the software you are using can save or export its files to this format so they can be used by co-designers and technicians who may be working with different software.

Vectorworks
(https://www.vectorworks.net)

The software comes with eight options, each aimed at a different set of users. *Vectorworks Spotlight* is aimed specifically at set and lighting designers in the entertainment industry, and has become a serious rival to *AutoCAD*. It is available for both Windows and Mac platforms, has excellent capabilities for draughting, 3D modelling and rendering, and can also be used to create documentation such as light plots. However, the learning curve is fairly steep for those wishing to use its more advanced features. The package also includes a digital image library named *Vision*, which contains a great many lighting, scenic and rigging items.

Vectorworks is not as expensive as *AutoCAD*, but is still one of the pricier packages. It is available by annual or monthly subscription with a 30-day free trial. A free educational version is available by submitting proof of academic status.

TurboCAD

(https://imsidesign.com/products/turbocad)

Long-standing CAD software distributed by IMSI Design that has gained considerable popularity over the years. It is available in several versions for Windows or Mac platforms. It is less expensive than *AutoCAD* or *Vectorworks* but the more advanced versions contain many of the same functions. Educational versions are available at 20 per cent or more off the standard prices. These are the same products as the full-priced versions, and the licences are perpetual rather than annually renewable. Fifteen-day free trials are also available.

Versions

TurboCAD Designer: A comparatively inexpensive 2D draughting program.

TurboCAD Deluxe: Comes with the addition of 3D modelling and rendering capabilities at a moderate price.

TurboCAD Professional: Has additional professional facilities and comes with an *AutoCAD*-style interface at a somewhat higher cost.

TurboCAD Platinum: Has more advanced draughting tools with 3D modelling and rendering facilities, plus many other special features. Unsurprisingly this is the highest-priced version.

BricsCAD

(https://www.bricsys.com/bricscad)

A draughting and 3D modelling program from Bricsys, a multinational software company based in Belgium. It operates on both Windows and Mac systems, with a simple and generally intuitive user interface. *BricsCAD* is available in five versions, but the following are of most interest to stage designers:

BricsCAD Lite: A concise 2D draughting program available for a comparatively inexpensive yearly subscription.

BricsCAD Pro: A 2D draughting plus 3D modelling and rendering program that also contains a materials library. It is available for a moderately priced yearly subscription. A 30-day free trial is available, and an educational licence is free for one year.

ProgeCAD

(https://www.progesoft.com)

ProgeCAD is a considerably less expensive alternative to *AutoCAD*, though some of the more advanced features are lacking. Users familiar with *AutoCAD* will find the interfaces almost identical, so should be able to use it immediately. It has similar 3D capabilities to *AutoCAD*, and saves to DWG format by default. A 30-day free trial is available, and an educational licence is free for one year. It is available for Windows only.

FreeCAD

(https://www.freecad.org)

A completely free, open-source draughting and 3D modelling program that operates efficiently on both Windows and Mac systems. It lacks some of the more advanced features that theatre designers may want, and the interface is somewhat basic and unintuitive, but there are many helpful tutorials available on YouTube. Files are saved to its own specific format, but can be imported and exported to most formats, including DWG.

SketchUp

(https://www.sketchup.com)

A series of comparatively low-priced, easy-to-use draughting and 3D modelling programs available by subscription from Trimble Inc. There is also a simpler, completely free version, but Trimble specifies that this is not to be used for commercial work. A seven-day free trial of *SketchUp Studio* is available, and there are reduced-price educational versions.

Versions

SketchUp Go: A low-priced, fairly basic program useful for viewing and editing existing models.

SketchUp Pro: The most popular version, with draughting and 3D modelling capabilities at a moderate cost.

SketchUp Studio: A more advanced version (note: available for Windows only) with advanced tools for creating animations and panoramas. This is the most expensive version, but still moderately priced when compared with similar packages from other providers.

SketchUp Studio for Students, or **SketchUp Studio for Educators**: These are comparatively inexpensive.

All versions come with access to a library of 'Photoreal Materials'.

3D MODELLING SOFTWARE

Most CAD software contains some 3D modelling capabilities, although often only in their more advanced (and more expensive) versions. However, the following packages are dedicated specifically to 3D modelling and CGI. They are not recommended for creating two-dimensional technical drawings of the kind required by theatre designers for printing to hard copy.

3ds Max

(https://www.autodesk.com/products/3ds-max)

A 3D modelling, animation and CGI program from Autodesk Inc., the same corporation that produces *AutoCAD*. It contains many advanced functions that seem to be aimed mainly at games developers, but are also useful to theatre designers. (Note: this software runs on Windows only.)

It is available from Autodesk Inc. by annual subscription, with a 30-day free trial. As with all Autodesk products, if you are a student or otherwise involved in education, you can access a free educational version with a twelve-month renewable licence. To obtain it, go to the 'Autodesk Education Community' page on the Autodesk website, and create an account. You will then need to verify your educational status by providing some appropriate documentation such as a student ID.

Rhino

(https://www.rhino3d.com)

A fully featured and comparatively easy-to-learn 3D modelling program that is particularly good at creating irregular or organic objects by the intuitive use of NURBS ('non-uniform rational basis splines'). It is available in both Windows and Mac versions.

A comprehensive series of user guides and tutorials is freely downloadable from the 'Support' page of the website, which can be a great help in evaluating the program before purchase.

The commercial version does not expire, and is available as a one-time purchase. An educational version, which is the same as the commercial version but at a considerably reduced price, is available with proof of status. There is also a free 90-day trial version.

Blender

(https://www.blender.org)

Constantly under development and maintained by the non-profit Blender Foundation community, *Blender* is a completely free, open-source, fully functional program for 3D modelling, rendering, animation and video creation. It will work on all operating systems, and has a truly spectacular range of capabilities, including the ability to render

A Digital Teapot

The 'Utah teapot' was created by Martin Newell, a computer graphics researcher at the University of Utah in 1975 – hence its name. Based upon his wife Melitta's teapot, he designed it for use when testing developments in 3D graphics, and because of its irregular curves, the negative space defined by the handle, and the shadow the handle casts upon the round pot, it proved to be an excellent experimental model.

It became something of an 'in' joke to hide a Utah teapot in unexpected places in animated videos, such as the brief tea-party scene in the film *Toy Story* and The Simpsons' *Teahouse of Horror* episode.

The 3D printable Utah teapot in the photograph was designed by Nik Clark and is available as a free download from *The Thingiverse* (https://www.thingiverse.com/thing:852078). The original teapot is now on display in the Computer History Museum in Mountain View, California.

The Utah teapot.

and animate fluids and atmospheric elements such as smoke and mist. Unfortunately it has a non-standard user-interface that some find a little difficult to master, but it is well worth the effort.

The animated film *Flow*, which won the Oscar for Best Animated Feature Film in 2024, was created entirely in *Blender*. See its trailer on YouTube (https://youtu.be/82WW9dVbgll) for an example of this free program's amazing capabilities.

MESHROOM
(https://meshroom.en.softonic.com)

This is not a program for designing three-dimensional digital objects from scratch, but one that will create them from a series of photographs of an actual object using a system known as 'photogrammetry'. About twenty to thirty good-quality photographs taken from many different angles are required, and the program then performs a sometimes rather lengthy analysis to create an editable 3D digital object. The interface is user-friendly, and the program is entirely free to download. (Note that it is currently available for Windows only.)

CAD FOR LIGHTING DESIGN

WYSIWYG
(cast-soft.com/wysiwyg-lighting-design)

This lighting design software from CAST in Toronto, Canada, contains capabilities for visualisation, plotting and virtual show control. It also comes with a huge digital library of 3D objects related to stage lighting. Unfortunately the software requires a rather clumsy dongle-driver to be inserted into a USB port and is designed primarily for computers running Windows – so carefully check compatibility before purchase.

The program is downloadable for a one-off payment or by yearly lease. A free educational version is available by submitting proof of academic status, and on graduation, students become eligible for a 50 per cent discount on their first purchase.

BITMAPPED GRAPHICS VERSUS VECTOR GRAPHICS

Almost all graphics software displays images in one of two distinct formats: 'bitmapped' (sometimes known as 'raster'), or 'vector' graphics. These two systems are used for quite different purposes: the bitmapped format can present subtly gradated, high-resolution photographic-style images in full

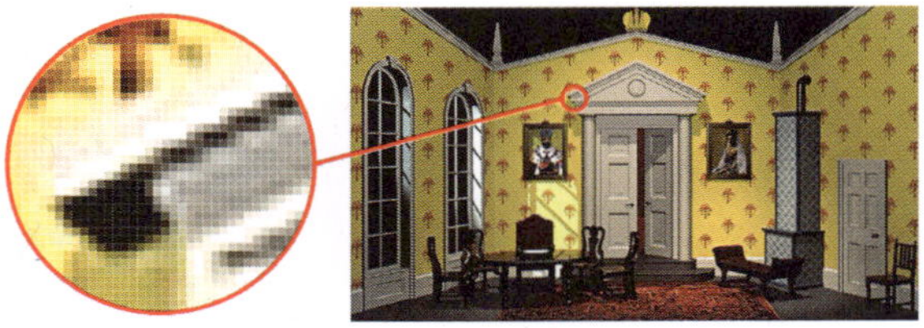

Bitmapped image revealing individual pixels when enlarged.

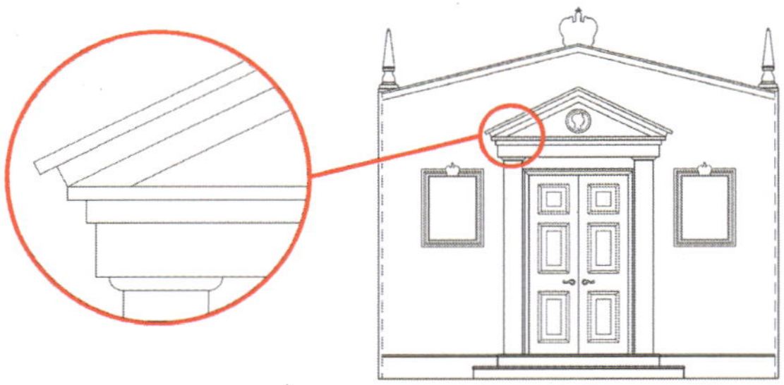

Vector drawing maintaining the integrity of lines when enlarged.

colour, whereas the vector format is used for images that may need to be reproduced in any size and where accuracy is a major consideration, such as stage plans and other technical drawings. The difference can be seen when an image is enlarged: the bitmapped format will show the enlarged individual dots or 'pixels' (picture elements) that make up the image, and any curved or angled lines will tend to become 'stepped' as the individual pixels become more clearly visible.

Picture quality is usually defined by 'DPI' (dots per inch) – the greater the DPI, the more a picture can be enlarged without noticeable degradation. 300 DPI is generally recommended for high-quality photographs, but for web images 72 DPI is the standard resolution.

A vector image maintains the integrity of its lines, even when very greatly enlarged, by creating algorithms to define each individual line or shape, including line width, colour and other qualities. As the length and position of each line is defined by plotting it from point to point, instead of as a fixed arrangement of pixels, the problem of pixelisation is avoided when the distance between plotting points is changed. This makes it the ideal format for technical drawings that are required to be displayed or printed to hard copy at any size, and it is therefore used by almost all CAD applications. It is also the format used to create shapes for conversion to three-dimensional digital objects.

Bitmapped File Formats

When storing photographic or other complex images, a graphics program needs to remember the precise colour and the location of each individual pixel. This can take up a large amount of the available storage space, so most formats employ special techniques to reduce the size of their picture files. This usually involves storing any areas of the image containing an array of pixels of the same colour as blocks rather than as individual pixels. As computers can display many more colours than the human eye can distinguish, pixels that are very close to each other in colour value may be seen as the same colour, so they can be stored as part of the same block with no discernible degradation of the image. However, after working on an image for multiple sessions and re-saving it a great many times, an ever-widening range of colours may be viewed as the same, and some deterioration in picture quality may eventually become apparent. This type of format is referred to as 'lossy'.

Other formats use compression techniques that fully maintain the quality of the image, but inevitably result in larger files. Thus there is always a compromise between image quality and file size, so when working on an image for an extended length of time, it is a good idea to save it in a 'non-lossy' format (such as TIF) while work is in progress, then store it in a compressed or 'lossy' format (such as JPG) when the final version has been reached.

Many graphics programs have developed their own proprietary file formats, but can usually export images to the following more common formats:

JPG or **JPEG** (Joint Photographic Experts Group – pronounced 'jay-peg'): A lossy format, but because of its ability to greatly reduce file sizes while retaining a reasonable image quality, it is by far the most popular format for storing photographic images. This is the standard format used by digital cameras and for displaying images on websites.

TIF or **TIFF** (Tag Image File Format): A versatile format used for storing high-quality images. This uses a non-lossy compression format that maintains the full integrity of the image, but is not capable of reducing file sizes to the same extent as JPG.

PNG (Portable Network Graphics – pronounced 'ping'): A format with a non-lossy compression technique that supports transparencies. A 'transparent' background is particularly convenient when lifting an irregularly shaped element from its background colour to be pasted into another image, which makes it a popular alternative to JPG, particularly for use on websites.

GIF (Graphics Interchange Format – pronounced with either a hard or a soft 'G'): A non-lossy format, normally limited to a palette of 256 colours, that also supports transparencies, and is particularly useful for comparatively simple hard-edged images such as logos, that contain sizeable areas of flat colour. It is not suitable for photographs, but is very popular for small animations such as animated emojis.

Vector Graphic File Formats

As vector graphics cater to more specialised requirements, many programs have their own specific file formats. Some attempts have been made to create a universal format, but a few proprietary formats remain by far the most popular, and can easily be imported or exported between most programs.

DWG (DraWinG): Originally created by Autodesk for storing 2D and 3D design data created with *AutoCAD*, but also the native format for several other CAD programs, and now probably the most popular format of all. *AutoCAD* also uses **BAK** (BAcKup) files to avoid duplicating file names when saving its automatically created backups, but these have to be changed to DWG to open them.

DWF (Design Web Format): A non-specific compressed file format developed by Autodesk that can be opened in many CAD applications, including *TurboCAD*. Surprisingly, however, considering its Autodesk credentials, files of this format cannot be opened directly into *AutoCAD*, although it is possible to import them into an open *AutoCAD* drawing using the 'XREF' command.

PDF (Portable Document Format): A popular format developed by Adobe for transferring and displaying formatted text and bitmapped or vector graphics files independent of the software and operating system used to create them. Adobe has a useful free 'drag and drop' PDF converter program that will accept text and/or graphic files in any format at https://www.adobe.com/acrobat/online/convert-pdf.html

GRAPHICS SOFTWARE

Listed below are three of the most popular software packages for the creation and manipulation of bitmapped and/or vector images.

Adobe Photoshop

(https://www.adobe.com/uk/products/photoshop.html)

Since 1990 *Photoshop* has become the most popular graphics program world-wide, in fact so popular that the verb 'to photoshop' is now to be found in *The Oxford English Dictionary*. The program contains a comprehensive set of tools for creating and manipulating bitmapped images that are especially useful for editing photographs.

Photoshop is downloadable for a yearly or monthly subscription, with a 50 per cent discount for the first three months, and a seven-day free trial. A reduced cost educational version is also available by submitting proof of academic status.

Affinity

(https://affinity.serif.com/en-gb)

Design software for Windows, Mac or iPad, consisting of the following:

Affinity Designer – for vector graphics.

Affinity Photo – for bitmapped graphics.

Affinity Publisher – for combining text and graphics to create page layouts.

The moderately priced one-time payment for each program, with no monthly costs, makes *Affinity* a serious competitor to other packages. Free trials are available, and there is an educational licence at a reduced price.

CorelDRAW Graphics Suite

(https://www.coreldraw.com)

This suite is a set of interrelated programs for creating and manipulating both vector graphics (*CorelDRAW)* and bitmapped graphics (*Corel PHOTO-PAINT*). A useful feature included as part of *CorelDRAW* is *PowerTRACE* for bitmap-to-vector image tracing. Also included is a sizeable library of clipart, digital photographs, fonts, fountain-fills and templates. *CorelDRAW* can be used to create technical drawings such as stage plans, but lacks most of the dedicated features contained in programs such as *AutoCAD.*

It is downloadable for a moderately priced yearly or monthly subscription, with a fifteen-day free trial. An educational version at a reduced price is also available by submitting proof of academic status.

VIDEO CONFERENCING

Although this is not CAD software, it is included here as it is virtually indispensable for theatre designers when working from home. Communication systems that allow users to see each other while talking are now commonplace, and most of us are used to video chatting with friends on our mobile phones. For theatre designers, video conferencing is particularly useful as we can use it to discuss our work with the director and colleagues, either individually or as a group, directly from our workplace.

It is also possible to share drawings, demonstrate models, and sketch freehand on a shared screen in real time, but to do all this, the small screen of a mobile phone will hardly be adequate, so a tablet, laptop or desktop computer is essential, and a fairly large screen is advisable when sharing work with several participants at the same time. Most desktop monitors have built-in speakers but rarely contain a camera, so a separate webcam may have to be clipped to the top of the screen.

The most popular video-conferencing system overall is *Zoom Workplace* (https://www.zoom.com), which is reasonably intuitive to use, and comes with a wide range of special features. A completely free version is available that allows you to conduct video meetings of up to 40 minutes in length with up to 100 attendees. For professional users there are several pricing levels, all of them comparatively inexpensive.

Arranging a work-related video conference requires a more calculated approach than when just chatting informally with a friend. As theatre designers, a large part of our work involves the creation and presentation of physical appearances, so logically, this should extend to our own appearance on video. Here are a few basic points for consideration:

- Sit facing the camera, with your eyes at approximately camera level. Looking into the camera will give the impression that you are looking directly into the eyes of the person you are talking to, so if you are using a portable computer, it is important to raise it to eye level for face-to-face communication. A sturdy, adjustable computer stand designed for the purpose is most convenient for this, but a pile of books or something similar will also work. The term 'laptop' should not be taken literally here, because if you place your computer on your lap, the viewer will be looking up to your face from the level of your knees, which is not a flattering angle.
- Check the background: you don't have to show a perfectly neat and carefully ordered studio, but an unmade bed, for example, does not inspire confidence in a designer's efficiency. *Zoom* will allow you to blur your background, but this merely convinces your viewers that you are hiding something.
- If you intend to show items such as model parts or illustrations, make sure they are within easy reach and ready to be picked up, or, if they are in digital format, already open on your computer's desktop ready to be clicked on when needed to be shown in a screen-share, instead of having to stop to search for them while the meeting is in progress.
- Always test the microphone and camera before initiating a meeting, and if other people share your computer, check that they have not used image enhancements or an avatar at a previous *Zoom* meeting, because if they were not cancelled these settings they may still be in effect, and it is embarrassing to have to explain that, in spite of appearances, you are not a rabbit.

HARDWARE

Computer

For serious design work, a desktop set-up is recommended, with a fairly large high-definition monitor (a diagonal measurement of about 70cm is a convenient size for most home desks), and a curved screen will give slightly improved vision at the outer edges, especially on larger-sized screens. Most CAD software can be run on a laptop or one of the larger tablets, but the smaller screen soon gets very crowded, which means that a lot of scrolling is required to access all parts of the image, and a mouse is generally more convenient than a touch screen for this. However, a laptop has the obvious advantage of portability, which means it can be taken to production meetings, or can sit on the production desk at technical rehearsals – so owning both a desktop and a laptop computer is probably the ideal solution. A mobile phone is *not* suitable for CAD work.

These are the major system components for consideration:

CPU (Central Processing Unit): The most significant part of any computer, as it affects how fast the computer works. Most computers come with a 'multi-core' processor, which means it can handle several tasks at the same time – essential for efficient use of CAD.

GPU (Graphics Processing Unit): Specifically designed for speedy and efficient handling of digital imagery.

RAM (Random Access Memory): The short-term memory area where images are stored while in use. A large amount of RAM means that your computer will run more quickly and more smoothly, especially when handling two or more programs simultaneously. Most graphic design programs need between 4 and 8 GB (gigabytes) of RAM to run, and 16 GB is generally recommended, but for more advanced techniques such as 3D modelling at least 32 GB is advisable.

Storage: Digital imagery, especially in 3D, requires a large storage area. An NVMe SSD (non-volatile memory express solid state drive) offers a large amount of storage space with a much higher transfer speed than the traditional hard drive. An alternative device is the SATA SSD (serial advanced technology attachment solid state drive), which, although not as fast as NVMe, is less expensive and almost universally compatible, making it a good choice when upgrading an older system.

Note that these specifications are more or less the same as those needed for playing advanced computer games, so for the non-technically minded, a good gaming computer could provide a suitable platform – with some pretty lighting effects in the tower unit too!

Printer/Scanner

A desktop printer/scanner is an essential piece of equipment for theatre designers, not just for printing documents, but more particularly for transferring digital imagery to hard copy, and vice versa. It also means that multiple copies of hand-drawn imagery such as costume designs can be scanned for circulation, while the designer retains the valuable original artwork. A printer with high-capacity refillable ink tanks will soon repay the higher purchase price, as even with very frequent use, the inks last for a surprisingly long time and the need for frequent replacement of expensive ink cartridges is eliminated.

Stage plans and technical drawings are eventually required in 1:25-scale hard-copy format for use in places such as workshops and rehearsal rooms, and for this, access to a large-scale printer/plotter is needed. This is beyond the reach of most designers, because even if the cost is not prohibitive, the amount of studio space required can be a problem. However, printer/plotters that can print at a resolution of 2,400 dpi on to an A0-width paper roll are available for home use, and can also be used to produce large-scale hi-res colour prints of reference photographs and computer-generated imagery to be displayed on the walls of the rehearsal room.

3D Printer

For theatre designers, access to a 3D printer is virtually a necessity. *See* Chapter 4 for a detailed survey.

Cutting Machines

A machine that will quickly and accurately cut out all the flat parts of a set model sounds very tempting, but there are some issues to be considered when selecting an appropriate cutter. A laser cutter is the quickest and most efficient cutting machine, but these are expensive and require stringent safety precautions, including special ventilation, which means that they are generally not a suitable choice for the home studio.

Other cutting machines are available that cut with a blade, and are specifically designed for home craftwork. Theatre designers will want to use them for cutting out model parts from mounting card with a thickness of about 3mm, which is thick enough to be glued on edge when this is required, and represents the approximate thickness of a stage flat at scale 1:25. Not all machines can cut as deeply as this, so carefully check the cutting depth before purchase.

Cricut (https://cricut.com) makes a range of moderately priced smart cutters designed for home use. Not all models will cut as deep as 3mm, and when cutting a rigid material such as mounting card, the flat width they can handle is strictly limited, so check before purchase.

Silhouette (https://www.silhouetteamerica.com) also manufacture a range of smart cutters for home use. Most of the range can take rigid card widths up to 60.96cm with a cutting depth of 3mm.

A further serious consideration for theatre designers when contemplating the purchase of a smart cutter should be its practical value, because although it can cut out finely detailed parts such as fancy ironwork patterns or window frames, these could probably be created on a 3D printer, and simpler shapes are easy to cut from card using a craft knife and metal rule in the usual way. So will the contribution that a cutting machine would make to your work justify its cost and the space it would take up in your work space?

Camera and Tripod

Most of us carry a versatile and remarkably efficient digital camera with us most of the time in our mobile phones, but whatever type of camera is used, a designer will find many situations, particularly when taking close-up photographs of set models, when a tripod is more or less essential to maintain the camera's precise position through multiple trial shots. A remote control is also a big help to prevent jogging the camera when pressing the shutter button.

Graphics Tablet

Many designers experience problems when drawing with a mouse, which can feel somewhat disconnected from the drawing appearing on the screen. Most laptop and tablet computers have touch-sensitive screens, which means that a stylus may be used to draw directly on to the screen, but when using a desktop computer, probably the best solution is to buy a graphics tablet. Wacom, the Japanese firm primarily involved in their development and manufacture, first started marketing graphics tablets for home use in the 1990s; since then, other firms have added to their development and they have become very efficient design tools, with a wide range of prices.

The most expensive versions are sophisticated pieces of hardware that come with large, touch-sensitive screens and specialised software that allows the user to select the type of drawing or colouring instrument and the type of surface to be simulated. When in use they have very much the same feeling as drawing naturally, and the results can look just like hand-drawn images. However, for use merely as a more natural-feeling alternative to drawing with a mouse, one of the simpler models that uses the computer's own screen and provides just a touch-sensitive drawing pad and cordless stylus, can work very effectively. The technology is seductive, but designers should bear in mind that similar results can be obtained by scanning a conventional drawing made with a pencil on paper.

A Desk Chair

Computers should come with a health warning: 'Prolonged usage may result in spinal problems and repetitive strain injuries.' So as you will probably be spending many working hours sitting at your computer, it is worth investing in a good, ergonomically designed desk chair with comfortable arm-rests and adequate back support.

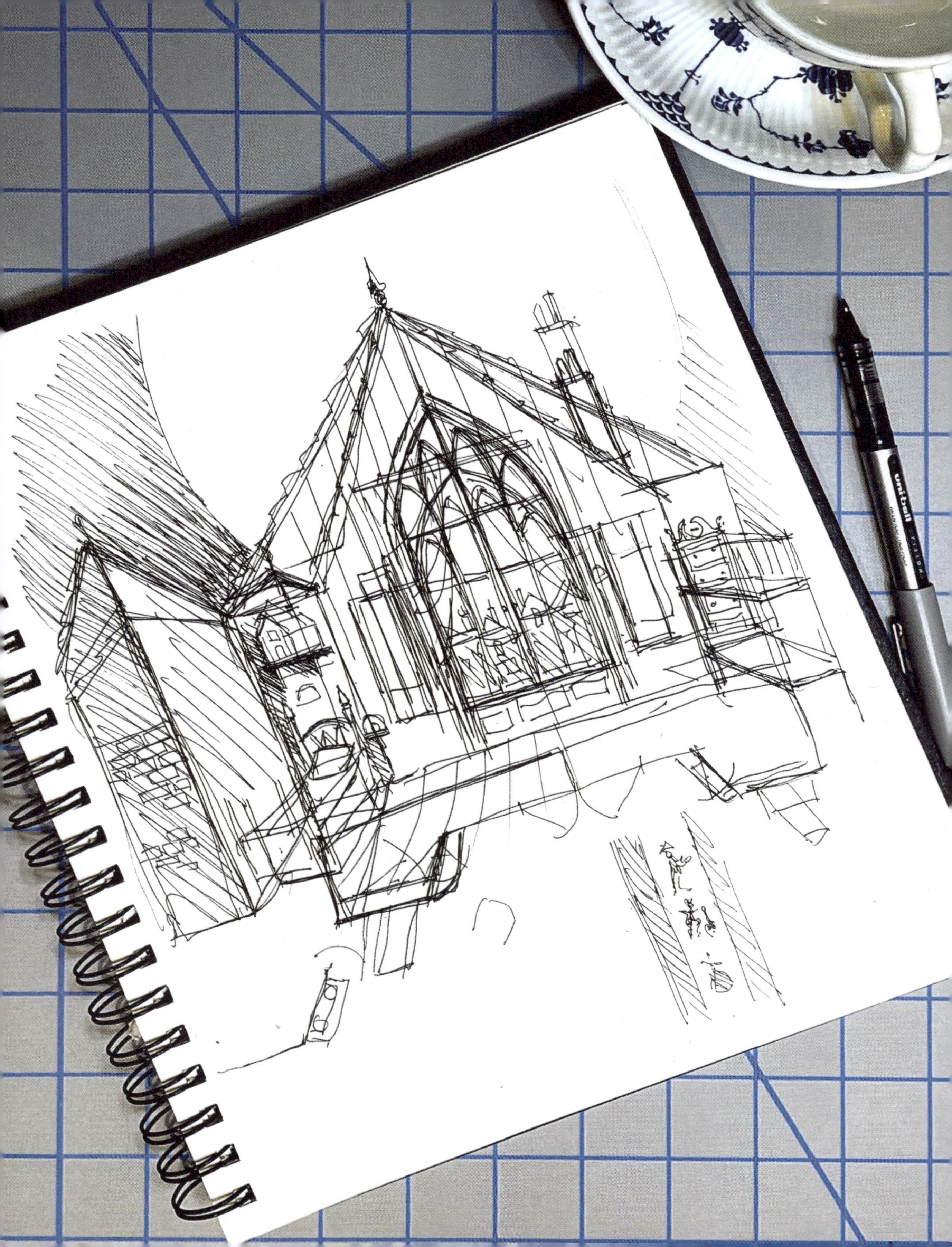

2

FROM SKETCHBOOK TO CAD

Most design processes begin with rough sketches of some kind. In theatre design they will probably be made on reading the script or during preliminary conversations with the show's director. These sketches may be very rough indeed and have little meaning to anyone apart from the designer, but as they represent the birth of a design concept, it's a good idea to keep them at hand for reference and as a possible source of re-inspiration throughout the entire process.

The scribbled sketch below was made during an early discussion with Ann Hodges, the show's director, for a production of *Shakespeare's Dog* by Rick Chafe at the Timms Centre for the Arts in Edmonton, Canada.

The set designer's task is to create a three-dimensional environment, not just a flat stage picture, so if the preliminary sketches do not include some indication of a plan, this should be introduced, even at this very early stage, to enforce consideration of the third dimension. A practical technique that may be employed here is to tape a sheet of paper immediately below a front-view sketch and rapidly scribble a plan on it, at roughly the same scale, referring to the sketch above. Obviously this technique can also work in reverse: to create a preliminary front view from a sketched plan. Accuracy will be introduced later, but at this conceptual stage, flexibility is more important.

The next step is to adapt the initial design concept to fit the specific performance space, and to do this it can be a big help to have a supply of A4 or letter-sized prints of the stage plan to sketch on. If the plan is available in a digital format such

First rough sketch of the set for *Shakespeare's Dog*.

Preliminary sketch for the Nursery scene in *Peter Pan.*

as DWG, small-scale prints can easily be produced from a desktop printer by first trimming the plan to the actual stage area, excluding any seating or off-stage elements, then hitting the 'fit to page' button when printing (*see* opposite).

If the plan is only available as large-scale hard copy, it can be scanned in sections of a size convenient for your scanner, then reassembled with bitmapped graphics software, and finally reduced to fit on to a page of a convenient size for your printer. The extreme sightlines should be indicated, and a gradated scale should be added at the bottom, which can be cut away from a spare copy to use as a temporary scale rule when working on these small, random-scale plans.

The sketch plan of the set can now be loosely redrawn by hand on one of the small stage plans, adjusting it to fit the available space and adding more details (*see* page 30). You now have a rough

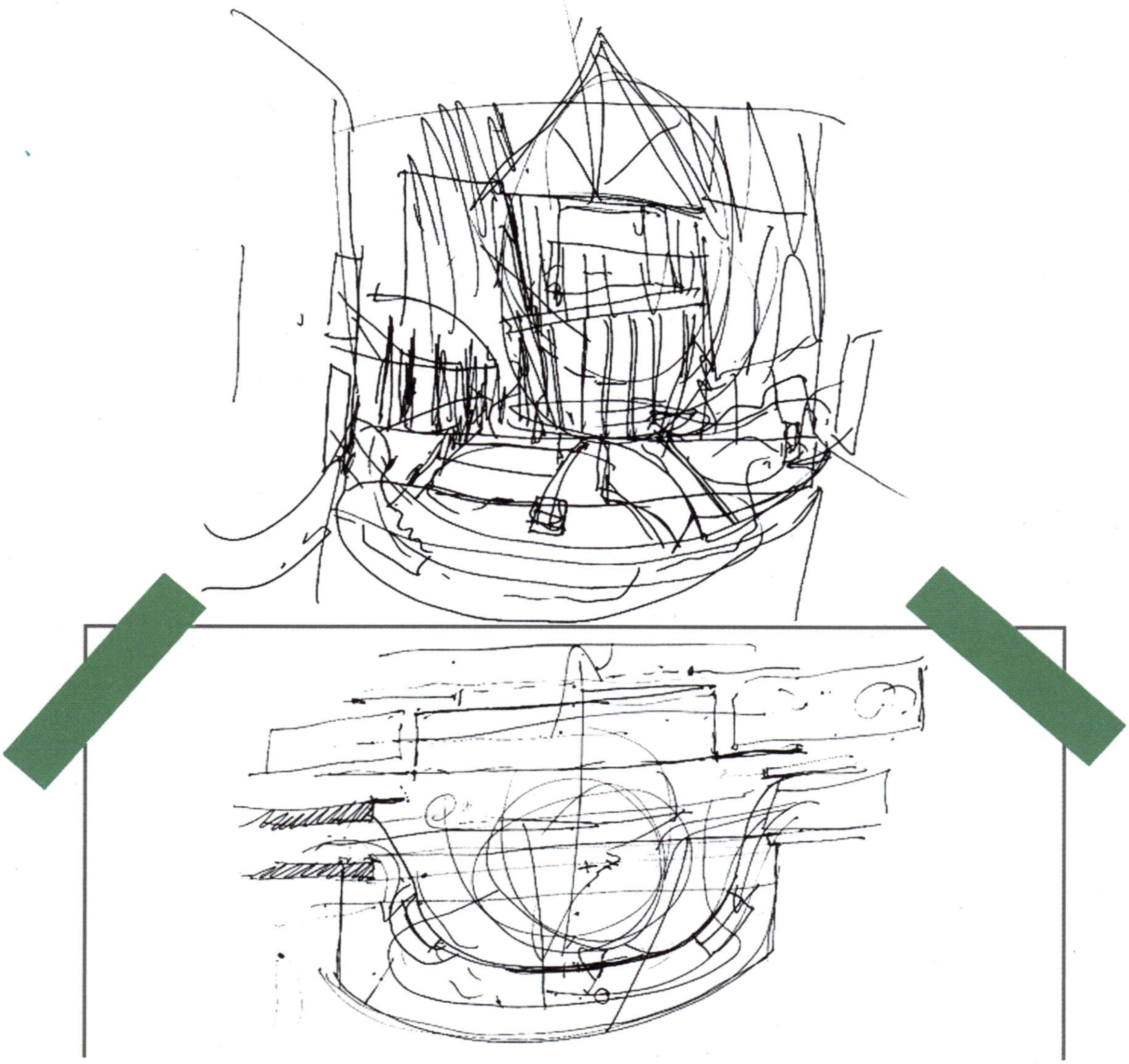

Rough stage plan based on sketched elevation.

plan of the set on the actual stage. It is still very imprecise, but ready to be reinterpreted and refined with your preferred CAD software. The rapidly executed, loose drawing style of a rough sketch is, of course, the direct antithesis of CAD, which is, by its nature, a precise and exact format, so a complete change of approach is needed when moving from sketches to computer.

It is convenient to introduce standard draughting conventions at this stage (*see* page 31), so the drawings will begin to take on a fully developed appearance that can sometimes be misleading if seen by other members of the production team. Avoid any possible confusion by prominently labelling each sheet as 'INCOMPLETE' in large letters until they reach their final version.

SETTING UP THE CAD WORKSPACE

This is not intended to be an *AutoCAD* instruction manual – plenty of those are available online or in books, but outlined here are some aspects that require particular consideration by theatre designers. First, a very important element that needs to be established before starting to draw, is the unit of measurement. Surprisingly, *AutoCAD*'s default unit is 'inches' – but expressed decimally! To reset this, click on the *AutoCAD* icon at top left of the work screen, and select 'Drawing Utilities', then 'Units'. The small panel shown on page 32 will appear, with pull-down lists from which you can select your preferred unit of measurement for both length and

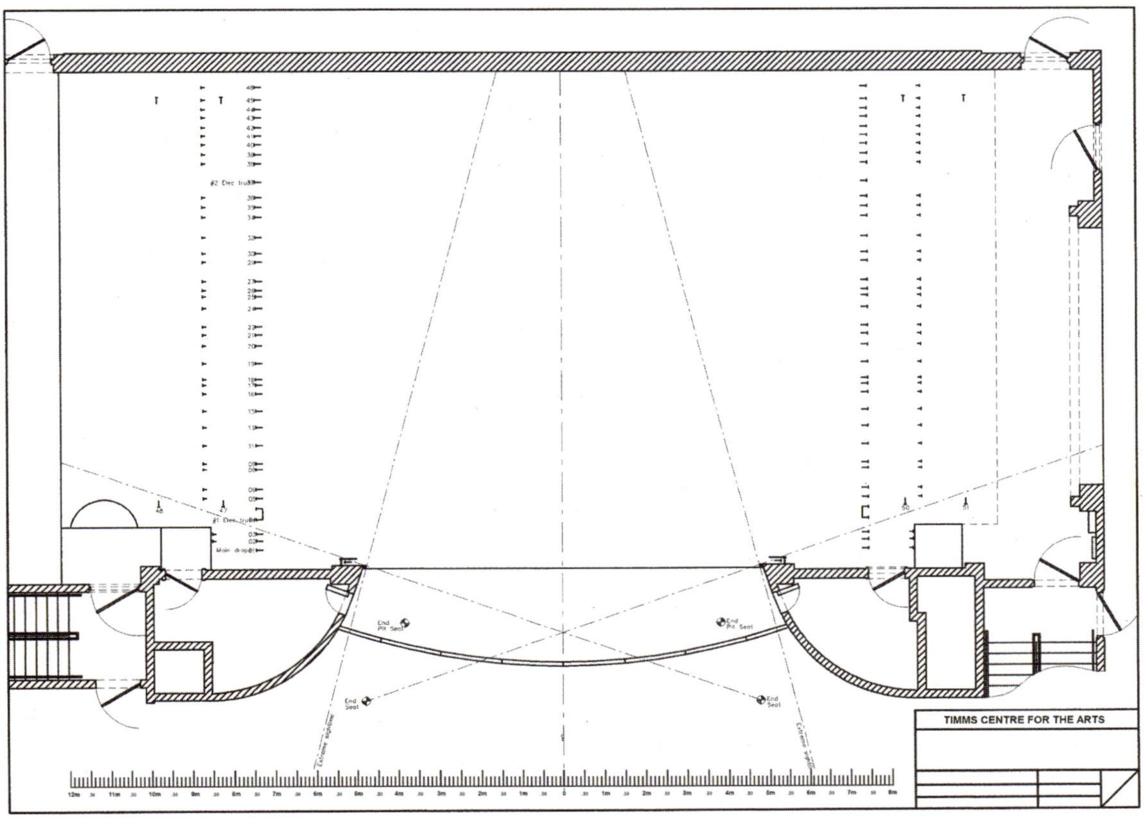

Plan of stage at the Timms Centre for the Arts.

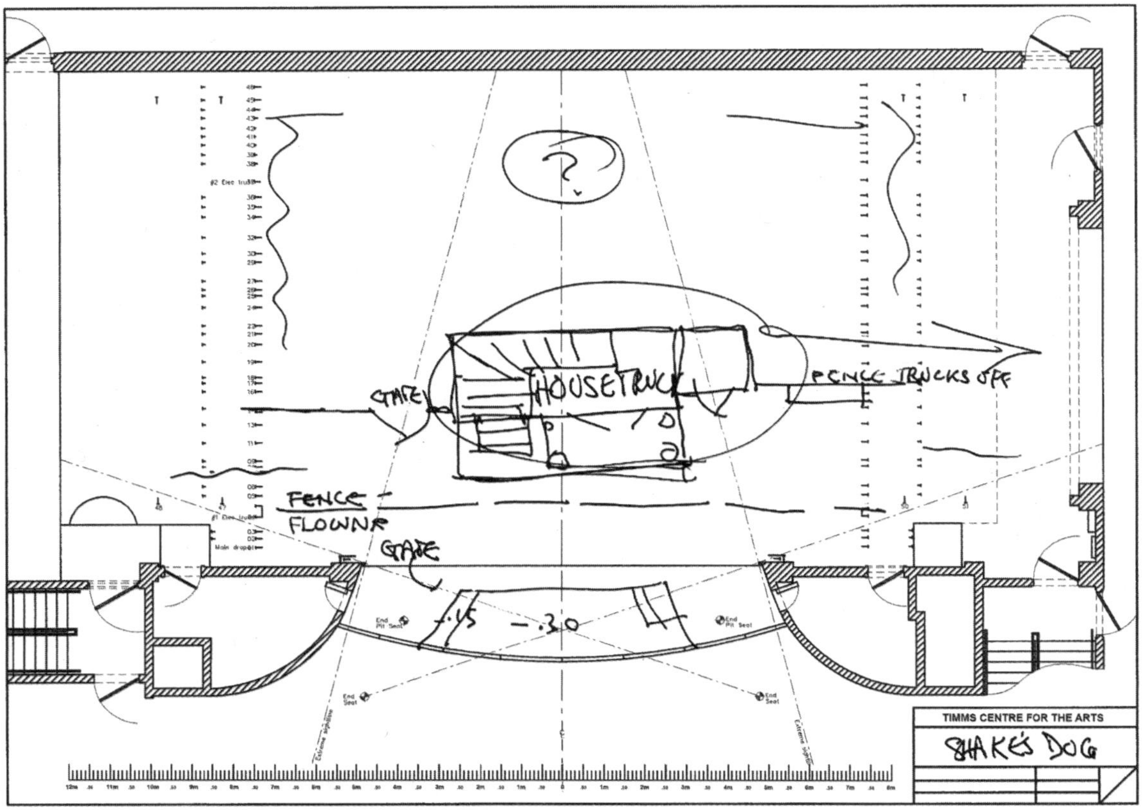

Rough plan of the set sketched on to an A4-size print of the stage.

angles. Selecting millimetres can produce some inconveniently long numbers in the dimension lines, so centimetres are usually preferable. You can also select the number of decimal places to be used for both length and angular measurements, and with centimetres selected, two places (0.00) are adequate for most theatre construction work.

The default *AutoCAD* work screen has a dark background, presumably to display a wide range of coloured layers more clearly, and to avoid the possibility of eyestrain which may result from working for long periods gazing at a brightly lit screen. However, now that LED monitors are standard, the problem of glare is greatly reduced, and as *AutoCAD* and most other CAD programs offer the possibility of completely reconfiguring appearance of the work screen to the user's personal preference, many designers choose to change the background colour to white or off-white and use black for all lines, changing the weight (thickness) and type (broken, dashed and so on) as appropriate, to make the on-screen image similar to a hard-copy version. All lines are usually automatically changed to black when the drawing is sent to a printer/plotter, but any that are required to be printed in their screen colour can be designated by selecting the little printer icon in the 'Layer Properties' menu.

To change the work screen's background colour, enter 'OPTIONS' into the command line; select 'Display' from the menu that appears, and click on 'Colors'. A pop-up menu will then allow you to select screen colours for any type of layout.

The chart on page 33 shows a suggested 'Layers' menu for use when working on stage plans and technical drawings: the 'Border' lines

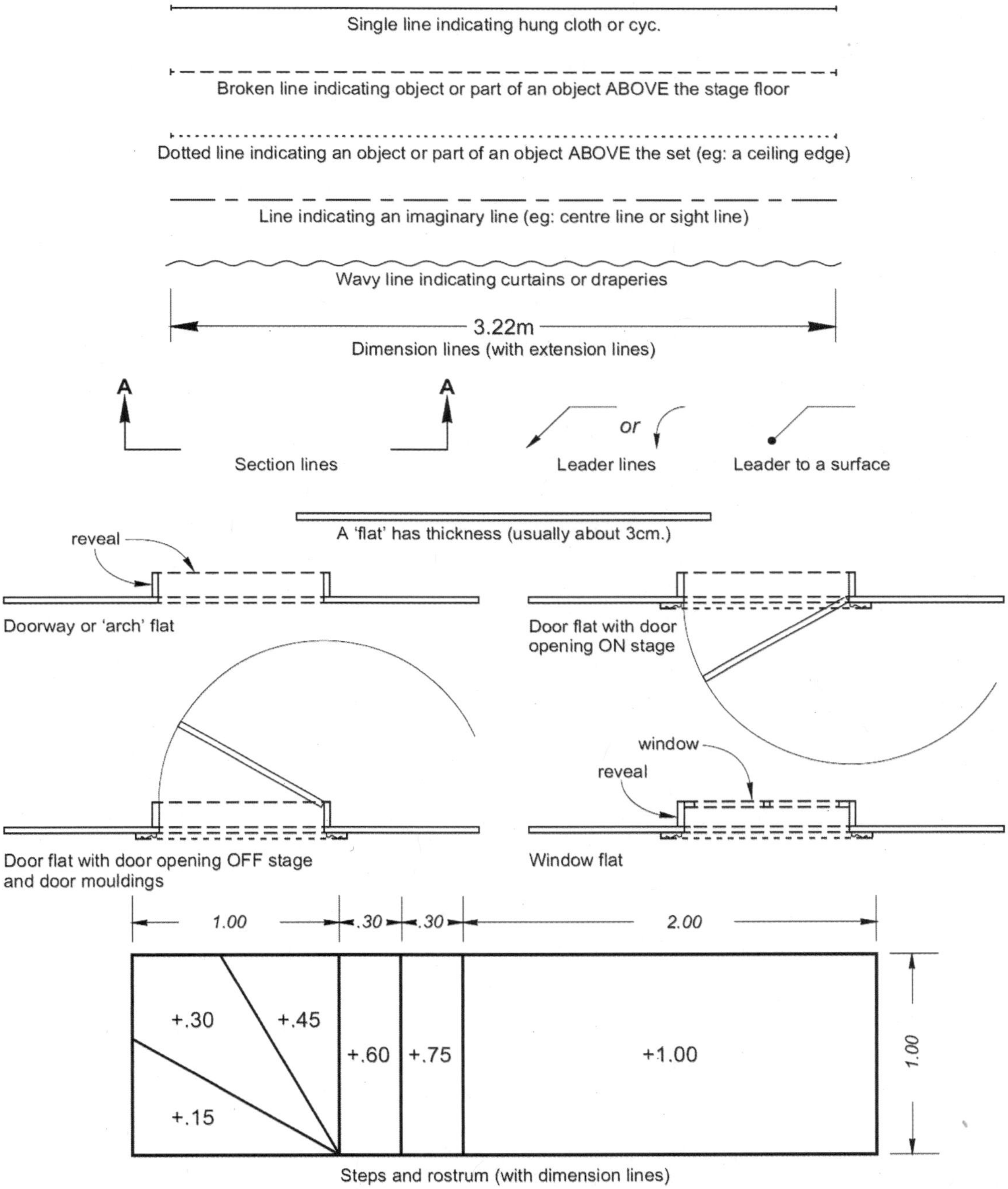

Draughting conventions for use on stage plans.

are thickest; 'Outline' has a standard medium thickness; and 'Fine lines', 'Dimension lines' and 'Sight lines' are the thinnest. Note that the 'Border', 'Centre line', 'Sight lines' and 'Stage' lines are intended to be permanent, so they are locked to avoid any accidental changes or erasures. All lines are black (250) apart from three 'Construction' layers, coloured red, blue and green, which are intended to be used for elements under development which, when complete, will be moved to their appropriate black layers.

Plan and Elevation

With constant reference to the rough sketches, an initial version of the stage plan can now be drawn in CAD, though many adjustments will inevitably be required and further details added as work progresses.

The CAD plan, even at an early stage in its development, can be used to construct a basic elevation of the set: first draw a horizontal base-line representing the stage floor, a little above the top border of the current drawing, then extend some temporary guidelines running upwards from corners and other significant points on the plan. The elevation suggested by the plan can now be drawn on the base-line using the extension lines as guides. Heights will need to be estimated, using the rough sketch as a guide, and taking into consideration the height available on the actual stage (*see* page 34, bottom).

The elevation can now be copied to a blank sheet and saved as a new file, to form the basis of a detailed full-page elevation. Surrounding elements and further details should be added next, gradually building up the complete set to give a good impression of how it will eventually appear on stage (*see* page 35, top). The figure on the right shows an actor of average height, included as an aid to visualising the scale.

When the plan and elevation have been draughted and the basic dimensions established, detailed working drawings for use by the set builders can be created (*see* page 35). These should show front or top views of all the set elements that are to be constructed, together with dimension lines and notes where they are needed. Several sheets of technical drawings are usually required for an average one-set show, including stage plan, two or three sheets of working drawings, and an elevation. A stage section, showing the full height of the stage above the set, is also useful, particularly to the lighting designer.

For a painted set it can be helpful to include a 'paint detail' layer in the working drawings with a clearly differentiated line type, to show where patterns and other paint details are to be placed. This provides a useful guide for the scene painters, and to avoid possible confusion, this layer can be hidden when printing out copies solely for construction.

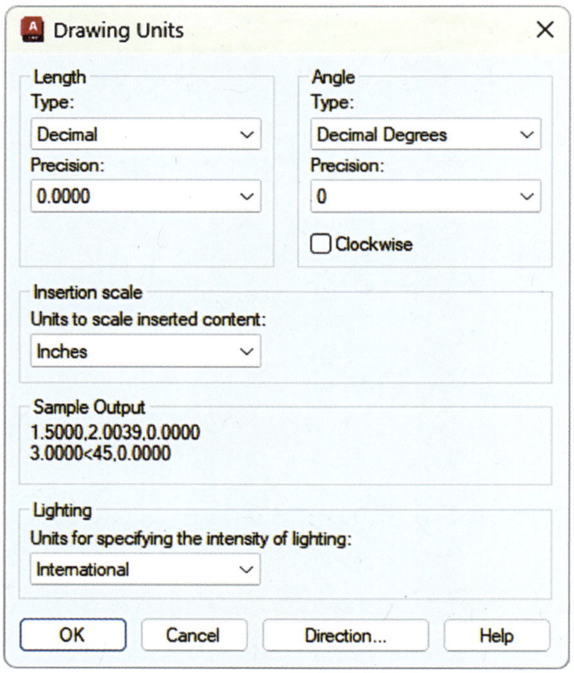

Defining measurement units in *AutoCAD*.

Status	Name	O...	F..	L.	P...	Color	Linetype	Lineweight	T...
	0					250	Continuous	Default	0
	Border					250	Continuous	0.50 mm	0
	Centre line					250	GENLT_6	0.09 mm	0
✓	Constr 01					10	Continuous	Default	0
	Constr 02					150	Continuous	Default	0
	Constr 03					92	Continuous	Default	0
	Defpoints					250	Continuous	Default	0
	Dimension lines					250	Continuous	0.09 mm	0
	Fine lines					250	Continuous	0.09 mm	0
	Fine lines broken					250	HIDDEN	0.09 mm	0
	Logo					250	Continuous	0.00 mm	0
	Outline					250	Continuous	0.25 mm	0
	Outline broken					250	HIDDEN	0.25 mm	0
	Sight lines					250	GENLT_6	0.09 mm	0
	Stage					250	Continuous	0.35 mm	0
	Stage drapes					250	Continuous	0.25 mm	0
	Text					250	Continuous	0.09 mm	0

Defining 'layers' in *AutoCAD.*

The title box (*see* page 36), usually placed at bottom right of each sheet, is particularly important, for it contains a large amount of information, such as the venue and the title of the show; the names of the director, set designer and lighting designer; the total number of sheets; and the number of that specific sheet. A wise designer also includes the date the drawing was created, as a defence against possible accusations of late delivery.

The version number is important when working in CAD, as it is easy to incorporate small changes and adjustments at a later stage, which might not be immediately apparent. So if drawings have already been circulated, the updated version number should give a warning that this sheet contains some significant changes from previous versions.

It may seem odd that no scale is indicated in the title box shown here, as this very important piece of information should be clearly displayed on every sheet of technical drawings distributed. However, as drawings are created at full size in CAD, the scale of any hard copy cannot be established until the sheet is actually being printed. The scale must therefore be added to the title box only immediately before printing (and removed from the

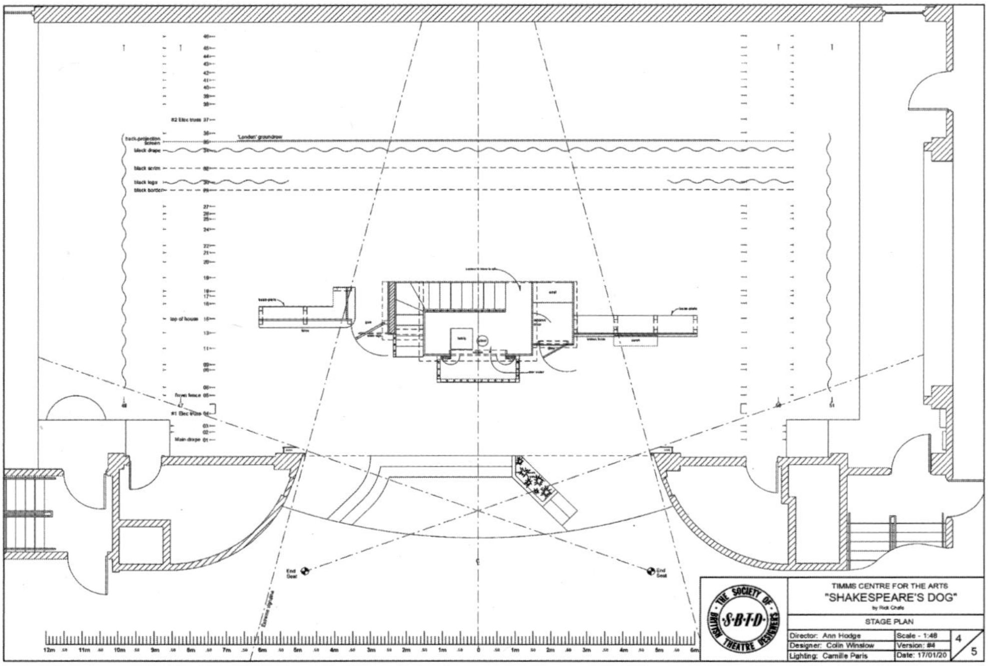

Complete stage plan developed in *AutoCAD.*

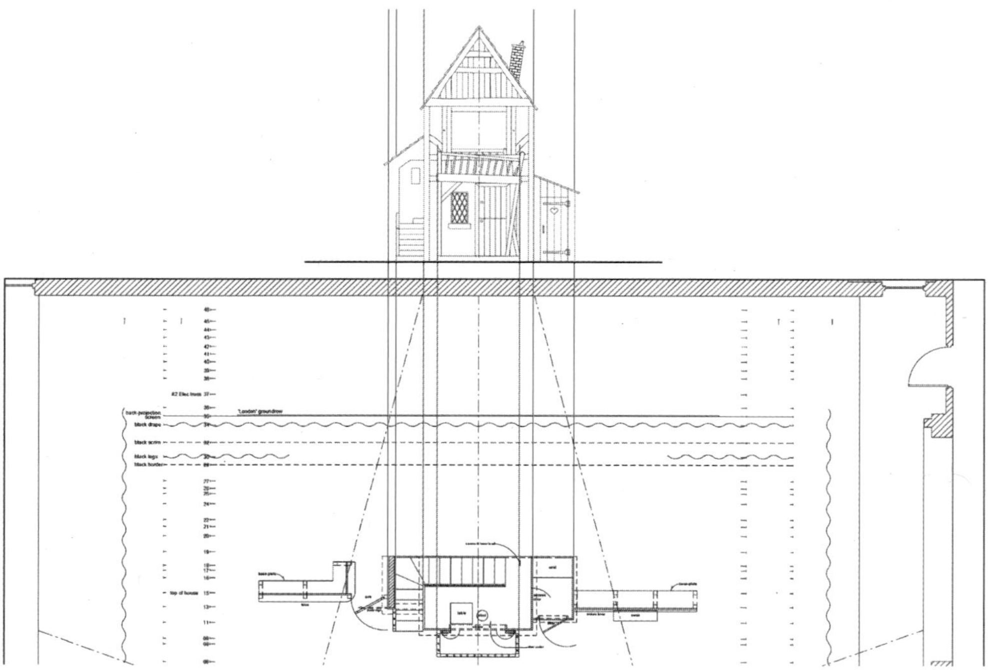

Elevation of the main structure constructed on vertical guidelines.

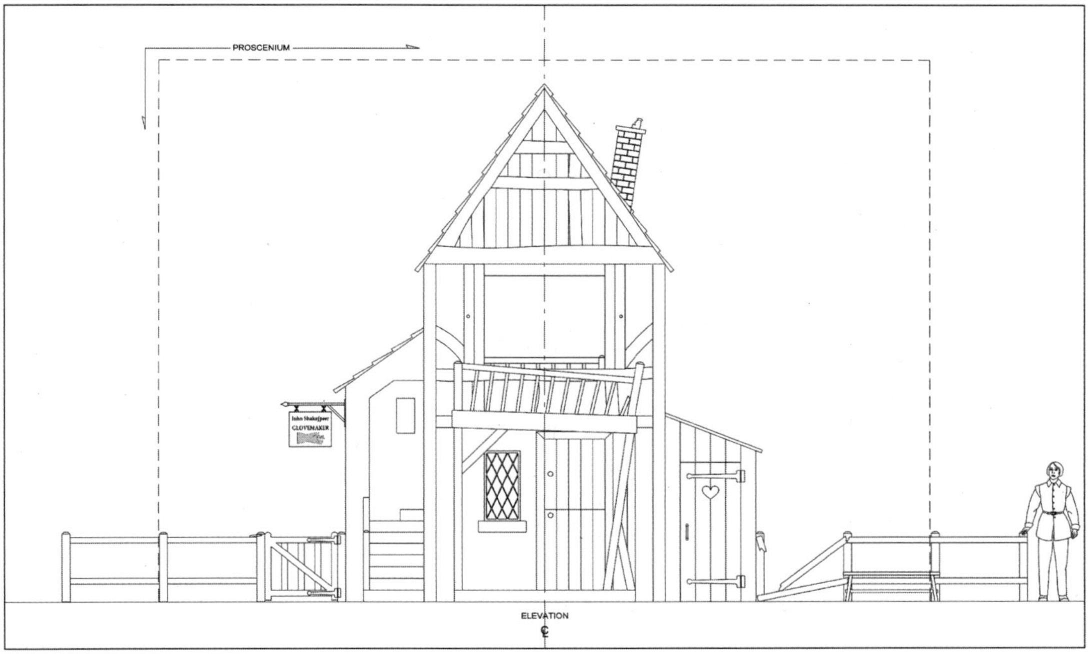

Completed elevation of the entire set.

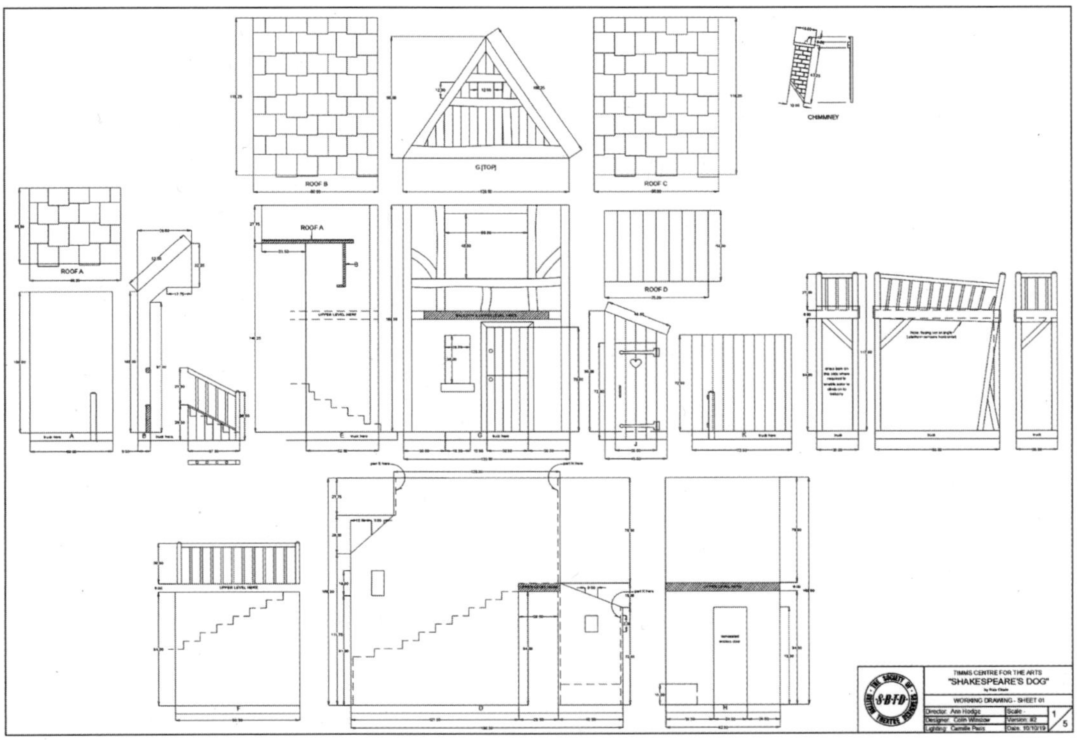

Working drawings developed from the elevation.

Working drawings including indication of paint detail.

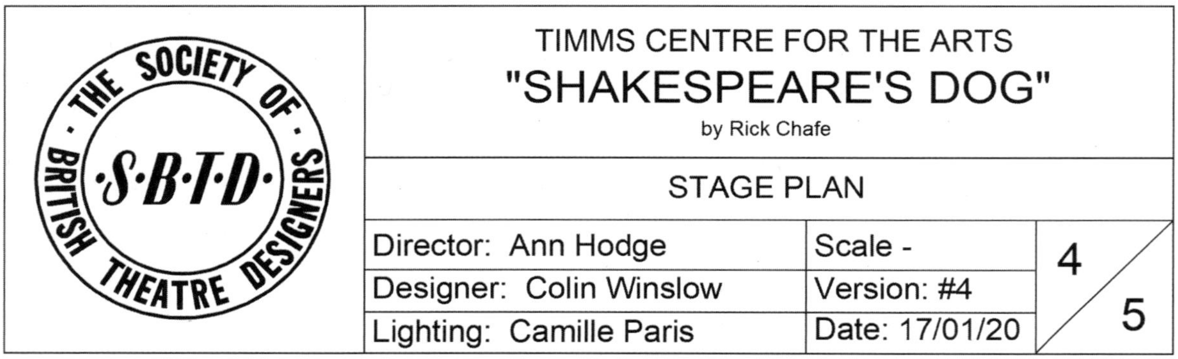

A typical title box.

stored copy directly afterwards to avoid possible future errors).

Sometimes, in an effort to economise on paper and maintain the integrity of line weights, the designer may have had a specific scale in mind and may have designed the drawing to fit a particular sized sheet (A0, A1 or A2 are usually the most convenient sizes) – but as the drawings may often be printed by people other than the designer, it is helpful to include a note in the show's digital folder, such as:

PRINTING THESE TECHNICAL DRAWINGS

The **PLAN** and the **SECTION** are intended to be printed at **scale 1:50**
Print them on an **A2** sheet for a convenient fit.
The **WORKING DRAWINGS** are intended to be printed at **scale 1:25**
Print them on an **A1** sheet for a convenient fit.

In the workshop, sheets of technical drawings are usually stored as rolls to avoid creasing, but when carrying them in a folder or a briefcase it is more useful to fold them with the title box conveniently displayed on top, as shown in the illustration. Folding drawings in this way has the added advantage that in a constricted area, such as in a café or on public transport, any part of the sheet can be examined without having to open out the entire drawing.

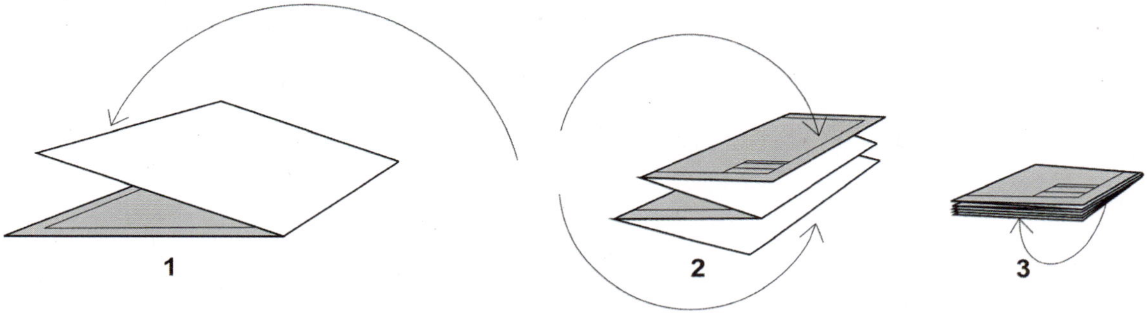

Folding technical drawings.

3
2D TO 3D

When the technical drawings are complete, and all the various set elements exist in two-dimensional form, it is time to start converting them to three-dimensional objects that can be positioned and combined to form a digital model of the complete set.

At this stage, most parts of the set will appear as a series of separately drawn straight or curved lines, linked or touching each other at the corners. To convert them to three-dimensional objects they must be viable two-dimensional shapes, not just groups of lines – so the outlines may need to be redrawn using closed 'polylines' or 'plines'. (The astute designer will already have used polylines for the main pieces when draughting the two-dimensional versions.) Note that it is important to first save the drawing under a different name so you can continue to work on this new version with no risk of losing the original.

It seems logical to begin with supporting structures such as rostra, steps or trucks, so first clarify the drawing by hiding any irrelevant layers such as 'dimension lines' or 'text', and create a new layer with a distinctive name such as 'rostra' and a colour that is roughly the same as that of the actual object. Using this new layer, trace over the object in the drawing with a continuous polyline, snapping to each of the corners and any other construction points, and finally 'closing' the polyline to create a viable shape. This shape can then be extended into the third dimension by 'extruding' it to the required height. (Remember that although you are building a model, in this case you are working at full size, and not to scale.) The extruded object can now be displayed on screen in a 'solid' format to give a reasonably good impression of the built piece.

Any walls that form part of a set will in reality be built as stage flats, so in the digital version they should be extruded to the thickness of a flat (approximately 3.5cm) rather than to the thickness of a real wall. Any cut-away areas, such as the door opening in the flat shown opposite, can be made by outlining the shape to be removed with a closed polyline, extruding it through the original object to a random height, and then 'subtracting' it.

To create the impression that stage walls have the thickness of real walls, the set builder will attach 'reveals', or thickness pieces, at the back of the flats around openings such as doorways and windows, so the digital modeller should employ a similar technique. In most stage rooms, windows are left without glass to avoid problems with unwanted reflections, so logically, the windows in the model also require no glass.

Built elements such as architraves, columns and finials can usually be constructed from several parts extruded to the appropriate heights with reference to the drawings, then fused together to make a single object. These architectural features

2D drawing and 3D rendering for *The Government Inspector*.

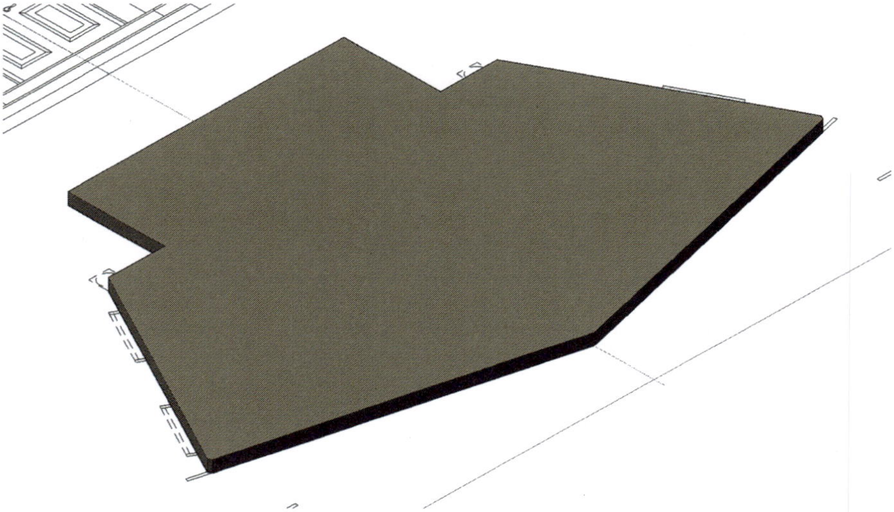

Platform extruded from a stage plan.

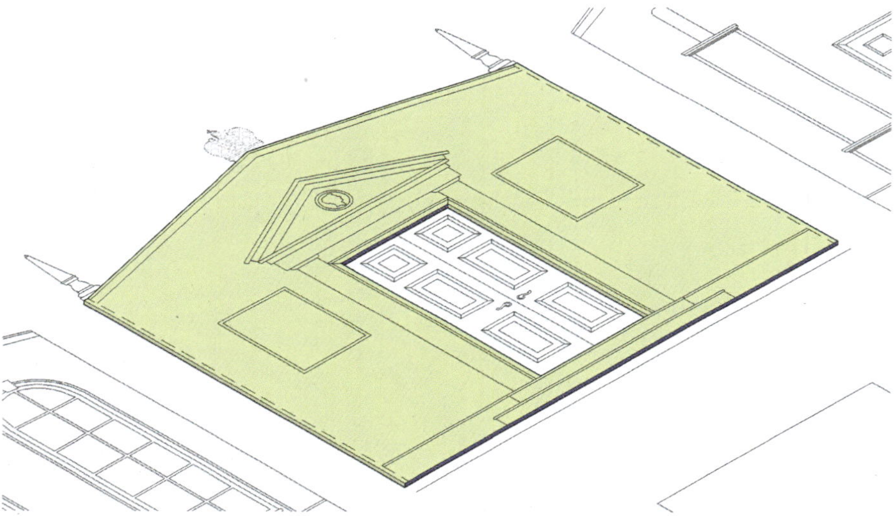

Scenic flat extruded from working drawings.

should be saved as individual objects so they can be reduced to scale and exported to a 3D printer format when constructing the physical set model.

When all the individual elements of the basic set have been digitally constructed, they can be moved to their correct position and orientation on the stage plan. This should present a good first impression of the finished set in three dimensions, although there are many finer details yet to be added.

Smaller objects such as furniture and set dressings can be added next. Detailed pieces of furniture, especially period furniture, can sometimes take a lot of time and effort to construct digitally, so all the pieces you make should be carefully stored in appropriately named folders for possible inclusion in future projects. In this way you can gradually build up your own digital props room.

For greater realism when rendered, surface textures, patterns and other qualities should be

Reveals added behind door and window openings.

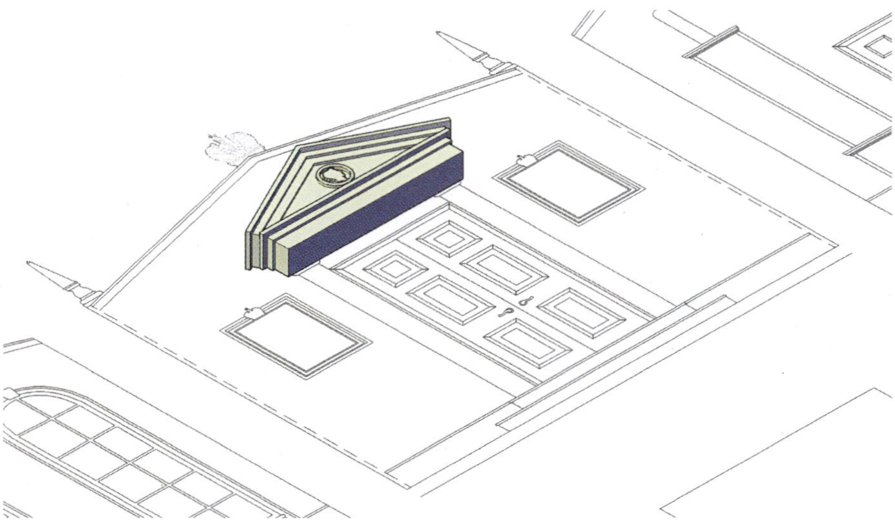

Architrave extruded from working drawings.

Low-resolution image of digitally assembled set.

Low-resolution image with furniture and set dressings added.

attached to all parts of the model. Most modelling programs come with a library of textures such as wood, stone, metal and glass, which can be used directly from the library or modified in various ways to create exactly the kind of surface required. Special patterns for decorative elements such as wallpapers or carpets can be created directly from the 'paint' layer in the working drawings or copied from reference material and added to the digital library. The patterns and other images shown below were created as bitmapped images especially for this set.

Repeating patterns, such as those used for the wallpaper and stove tiles, must be carefully designed to produce a continuous pattern when the image is placed immediately next to itself both horizontally and vertically. The size of these images is irrelevant at this stage, as this can be established when they are applied to their specific surfaces. For example, the painted detail on the 'house' flats at each side of the stage is greatly enlarged in the final rendering.

Bitmapped image applied to a sphere.

Specially designed bit-mapped imagery for use in a digital rendering.

Hi-res renderings with textures, patterns and simulated stage lighting added.

Production photograph of *The Government Inspector* at the Timms Centre for the Arts.

Note that a surface does not have to be flat to accept a bitmapped image – they can also be applied to rounded or curved surfaces, such as the map of the world in this rendering of an antique globe: see illustration on page 43.

In the final renderings of the set for Gogol's *The Government Inspector*, directed by Ron Jenkins at the Timms Centre for the Arts in Edmonton, Canada, it can been seen that some objects have both an image and a surface texture. The carpet, for example, not only has a distinctive pattern, but a rough pile texture has also been applied (*see* 'Bump Maps' below) and the tiles decorating the stove have a ceramic gloss on top of the pattern. Other objects, such as the stove pipe and door handles, have only a surface texture applied to a base colour – a metallic gloss in this case. These renderings have been greatly enhanced by digital lighting effects, which will be discussed later in this chapter. A production photograph of the real set in performance is included for comparison.

INCLUDING IMAGERY IN TECHNICAL DRAWINGS

Most CAD programs will allow bitmapped images to be 'imported' and displayed within a vector drawing, so CGI renderings may be added to a sheet of working drawings to show how the finished set should appear on stage. In *AutoCAD*, by using the 'IMAGEATTACH' command, images can easily be scaled to a convenient size and moved to a suitable position on the page, but to avoid confusion, they should be placed in a separate box and clearly labelled as a perspective rendering and therefore not to scale. The background colour on stage is generally black, so when a set rendering is to be included in a sheet intended for reproduction as hard copy, as in the example below, the removal of any large areas of flat black will improve clarity and save a considerable amount of printer ink.

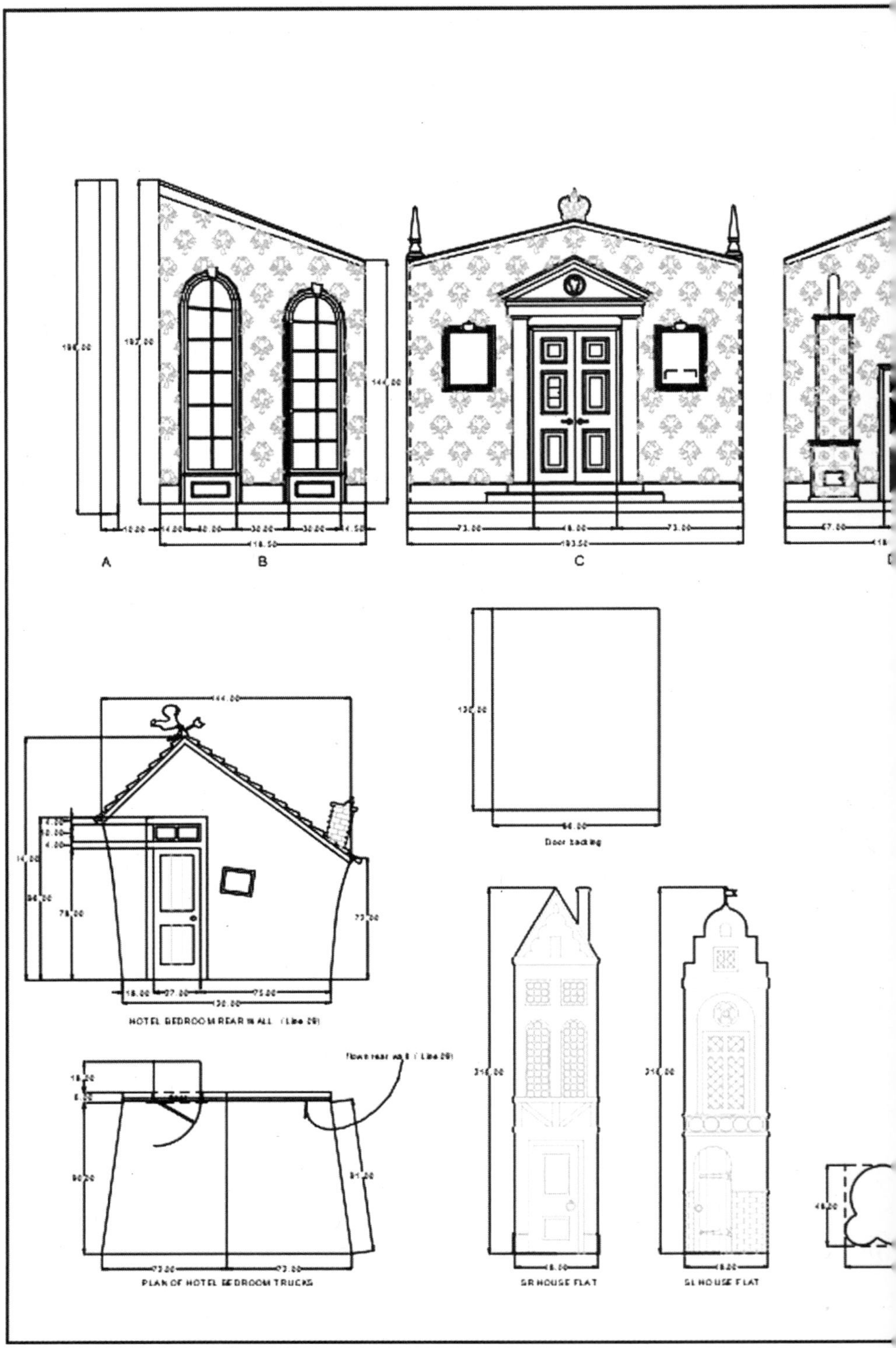

Working drawings with a perspective rendering of the completed set included.

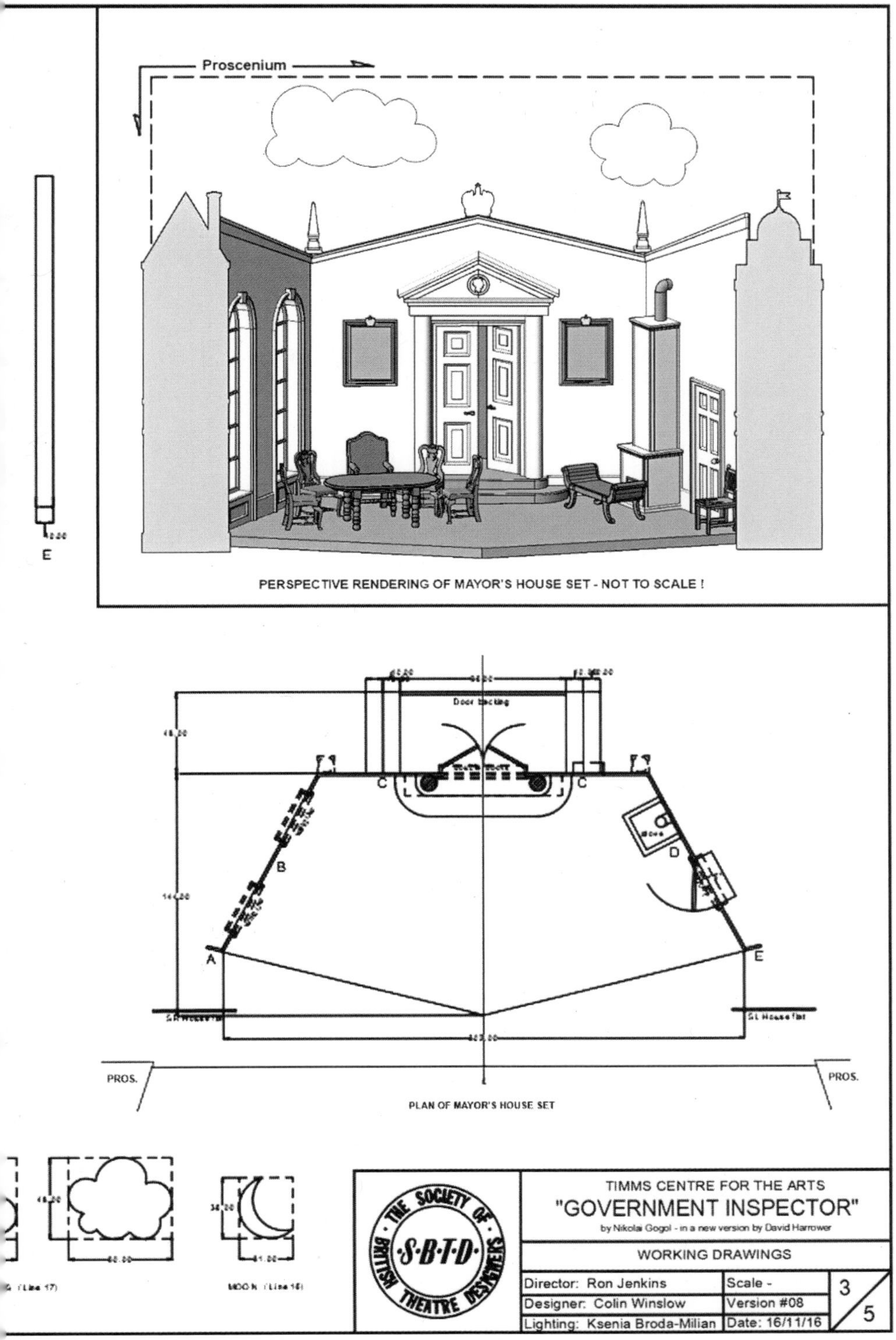
Proscenium
PERSPECTIVE RENDERING OF MAYOR'S HOUSE SET - NOT TO SCALE !
E
Door backing
C
C
B
D
A
E
PROS.
PROS.
PLAN OF MAYOR'S HOUSE SET
TIMMS CENTRE FOR THE ARTS
"GOVERNMENT INSPECTOR"
by Nikolai Gogol - in a new version by David Harrower
WORKING DRAWINGS
Director: Ron Jenkins
Scale -
Designer: Colin Winslow
Version #08
Lighting: Ksenia Broda-Milian
Date: 16/11/16
3/5
THE SOCIETY OF BRITISH THEATRE DESIGNERS
·S·B·T·D·

Going Too Far

Having gained a degree of proficiency in 3D modelling techniques, it is easy to get carried away with the technology and include details that are really quite irrelevant, but give some satisfaction to the designer. An example of this can be found in the digital model of the set for *Shakespeare's Dog* discussed in Chapter 2: the upper level represents the room where Shakespeare works, and on zooming in – beyond what would be visible to an audience – the viewer will discover on the table, a sheet of paper with the messily scrawled opening lines of *Romeo and Juliet*. This, of course, is totally unnecessary, increases the size of the file, is pure self-indulgence on the part of the designer, and *not* to be recommended.

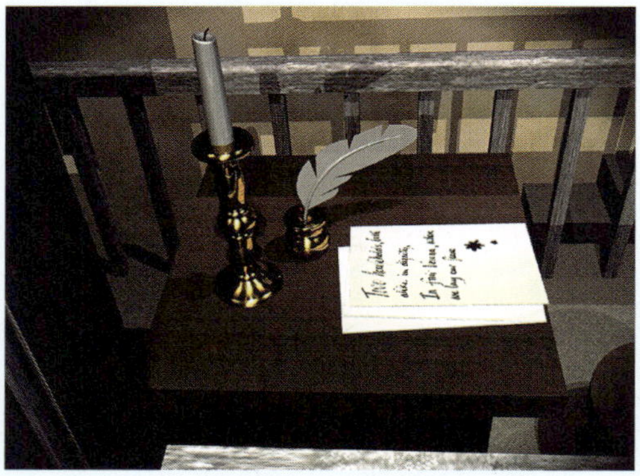

CGI of Shakespeare's writing table.

SHINY SURFACES AND REFLECTIONS

3D modelling programs are usually very good at creating shiny, reflective and transparent elements, including a naturalistic refraction effect where that is appropriate. All these qualities are quantifiable, so you can create, for example, a shiny surface that hardly reflects at all, or one that has a very high reflective quality, reflecting the objects around it like a mirror. In the renderings of the set for *The Government Inspector* on page 44, the polished wooden furniture has been given a high gloss finish that is also slightly reflective, and by comparing the two pictures, it can be seen that the software is also capable of adjusting the reflected image, depending on the angle of view.

The example [below] was created in *AutoCAD* as part of a set for Václav Havel's play *Largo Desolato*, which contained a sideboard and a shiny metal tray with a glass bottle and two tumblers. This involved a complicated interaction of transparent and reflective surfaces – all efficiently handled in this rendering.

Transparent, shiny and reflective surfaces created in *AutoCAD*.

BUMP MAPS

A 'bump map', or 'texture map', is used to simulate effects such as heavy grains, rough textures and indentations of various kinds. The use of a bump map gives the impression that the texture is actually incised three-dimensionally into a digital object, rather than being merely an image applied to the surface. The software's materials library will probably contain a selection of bump maps, but original versions can be created from scratch or adapted from a photograph using any bitmapped graphics software.

A bump map consists of a grey-scale image which, when applied to an object, will appear to sink into the surface. The darker toned areas will appear to sink more deeply than the lighter ones, so a variety of depths can be suggested by a single bump map. The overall depth of the incised texture can be further adjusted in the modelling program, and a coloured texture or pattern image may be applied over the bump-mapped surface to complete the effect. So, for example, a realistic deep-pile patterned carpet may be created by combining a bump map for the pile with a coloured image of the pattern, as in the renderings of the set for *The Government Inspector.*

The image below shows a detail from a CGI rendering of the stockade scene from a production of *Treasure Island* at Theatr Clwyd, in which a bump map has been applied to several surfaces to suggest the coarse grain of unfinished lumber.

CREATING SCENIC GAUZES

For the production of *Treasure Island* referred to above, the jungle scenes were created on stage with three full-stage drops hung two or three metres apart, and some prop plants and rocks set between them. The rear drop was made of seamless cotton sheeting, with trees and distant mountains painted on to it with opaque black paint. The other two drops were made from scenic gauze or 'scrim', with leaves and branches cut from painted canvas and glued on to them (*see* designs on pages 50 and 51). The translucent rear drop was lit from behind in various colours to create day, night or sunset scenes, as required, causing the trees to appear in silhouette against the sky. Actors could move between, and occasionally through, the transparent gauze drops, creating the effect of walking through heavy foliage.

The creation of a CGI version of this scene, with its very theatrical effects, seemed at first to be a daunting task, but the full-stage drops were recreated in *AutoCAD* from the scanned hand-drawn designs and given varying degrees of translucency, with tree trunks and foliage superimposed as thin solid objects. When rendered with appropriate lighting directed between and through the drops, the result was a reasonable likeness of how the scene eventually appeared on stage.

Bump map designed to simulate a heavily grained effect.

Use of a bump map in rendering a CGI.

Design for the backlit rear drop.

Mid-stage appliquéd scenic gauze.

Down-stage appliquéd scenic gauze.

CGI of the 'Jungle' set in *Treasure Island*.

LIGHTING DIGITAL MODELS

Most stages are dark interior spaces, so nothing can be seen without the use of artificial lighting. The main purpose in lighting a theatrical performance is to reveal the performers to the audience, but stage lighting is also used to reveal and enhance the acting space in a way that creates an emotional environment appropriate for the scene taking place within it. When lighting the digital image of a stage set, however, the emphasis is slightly different, for as there are no performers to be taken into consideration, all resources can be concentrated upon creating a realistic atmospheric image of the set.

Unfortunately, the light sources available in 3D modelling programs are not the same as the stage 'lanterns' or 'luminaires' used in real-life theatres, so somewhat different techniques have to be employed. CGI lights can be focused, coloured and dimmed, but in ways that are unrelated to real stage lighting. Two major differences are these: the light sources are invisible, so they can be placed anywhere in the acting area without causing an obstruction; and cast shadows are optional, so make sure they are switched to 'on' to get the maximum effect from your digital lighting rig. Any unwanted shadows can be turned off at a later stage – a facility that real-life lighting designers would love to have!

AutoCAD offers a choice of four types of light: point, spot, distant and weblight. Each of these lights is capable of being modified in various ways. When using the 'spot' light, for example, the user can specify its source; the 'target location' or direction; the 'hotspot' and 'falloff' angles, together with its intensity and colour. This is probably the most useful light for recreating stage lighting effects. The 'point' light is similar to a lightbulb, throwing out light in all directions, and can be useful set at a low level when creating visible light sources such as lamps and candle flames. The 'weblight' spreads light in all directions and can be used to boost the general illumination, but when starting to light a digital scene, it is particularly helpful to place a low-level weblight somewhere in the middle of the acting area, so that all the set elements are visible to some extent while focusing spot lights. The 'distant' light is designed to create an effect similar to sunlight, so is probably the least useful type in a theatrical context.

When the 'GLYPHS' command is switched on, icons appear in the model on screen to indicate the type of light in use and where it has been positioned. Glyphs are automatically eliminated when an image is rendered.

It is possible to use digital gobos when lighting a digital stage set in the same way as a lighting designer does when lighting a show in real life. First create the basic gobo by drawing a circle of about 10cm diameter and extruding it to about a millimetre thick. Then draw the shapes to be cut out: extrude them right through the disc and subtract them to create holes. Alternatively you could select a gobo

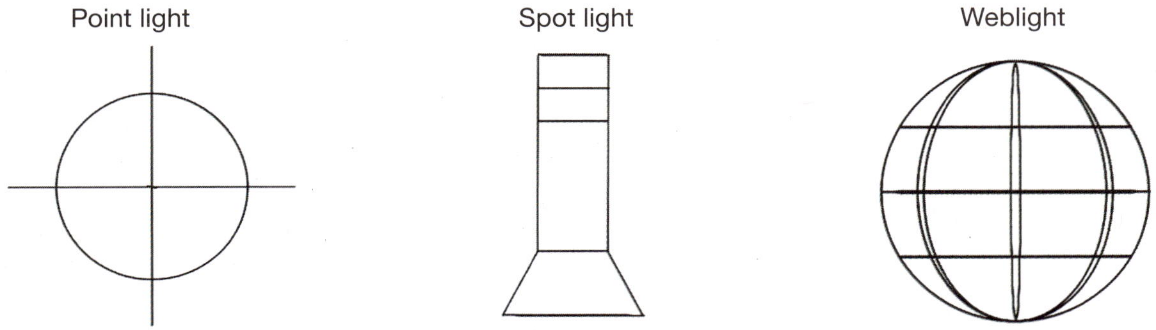

Lighting glyphs in *AutoCAD*.

Gobos

A gobo is a frequently used device in stage lighting that in its simplest form, consists of a disc of thin metal, varying in size from about 50 to 86mm in diameter, with some kind of design cut into it. When placed into the slot or 'gate' of a focusable spot light, the design is projected on to the stage. It is typically used to produce effects such as light striking through foliage or a window frame, or simply as a 'break-up' to add texture or a pattern to the light.

A gobo from Rosco.

from the Rosco gobo catalogue (emea.rosco.com/en/products/catalog/gobos) and import the image into a 3D modelling program. Then trace round the cut-out shapes and remove them as described above. This method has the advantage that the lighting designer can buy a real gobo that is identical to the one used in the digital model. It is also possible to have a real gobo made from your original design, but this may be expensive, unless you have access to a laser or 'smart' cutter that will handle metal.

Having created the digital gobo, position it in front of a digital spot light. Slight adjustments to the distance of the gobo from the light source can make big differences to the effect, so some time will need to be spent in trial and error to get just the effect desired.

The pictures below and overleaf show a digital gobo and the effect produced by it in a rendering of the 'Mirkwood' set for a stage version of *The Hobbit* directed by Graham Watkins at The Redgrave Theatre, Farnham.

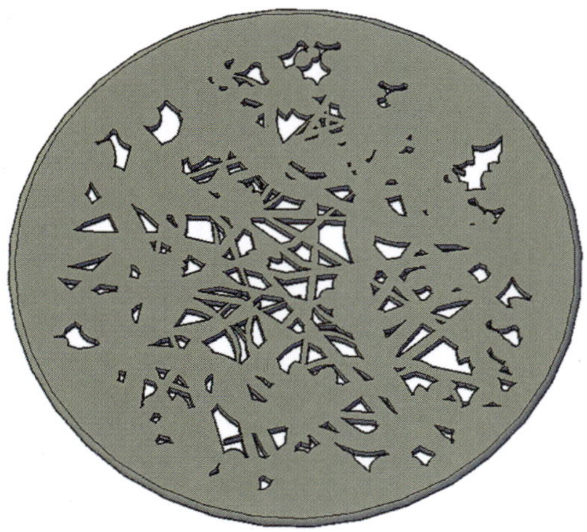

A digital gobo.

CGI of a set for *The Hobbit* showing the lighting effect from a digital gobo.

CREATING ATMOSPHERE

The opening scene of Chekhov's play *The Cherry Orchard* takes place at dawn in a room in a dacha where two of the characters are awaiting the return of Mme Ranevsky, the owner of the estate and the central character of the play. It is a scene that owes much of its visual impact to the skill of the lighting designer. Rendered only in outline, the digital set can be seen in the illustration below.

However, with the addition of appropriate lighting, and with patterns and textures applied to many of the surfaces, the set becomes much more atmospheric in the hi-resolution rendering seen in the illustration below and overleaf.

Here, a low-intensity weblight has been set at the centre of the stage to provide some general illumination, with another one, slightly brighter, directly over the table and chairs where Mme Ranevsky will sit. A weblight is also used upstage to light the sky-cloth. Two spot lights create the effect of the dawn light casting shadows of the window frames across the floor, and a point light is used for the small candle flame before the icon in the corner.

The wallpaper and stove patterns have all been specially designed, and the pattern on the plates is lifted from a photograph of an actual plate. The pictures and the icon have images scanned from art books, and the carpet pattern is taken from a catalogue and adjusted in *Corel PHOTO-PAINT* to obtain the tapered shape at the stage left side to align with the set's slight false perspective. The various woods, metals and velvet textures are all

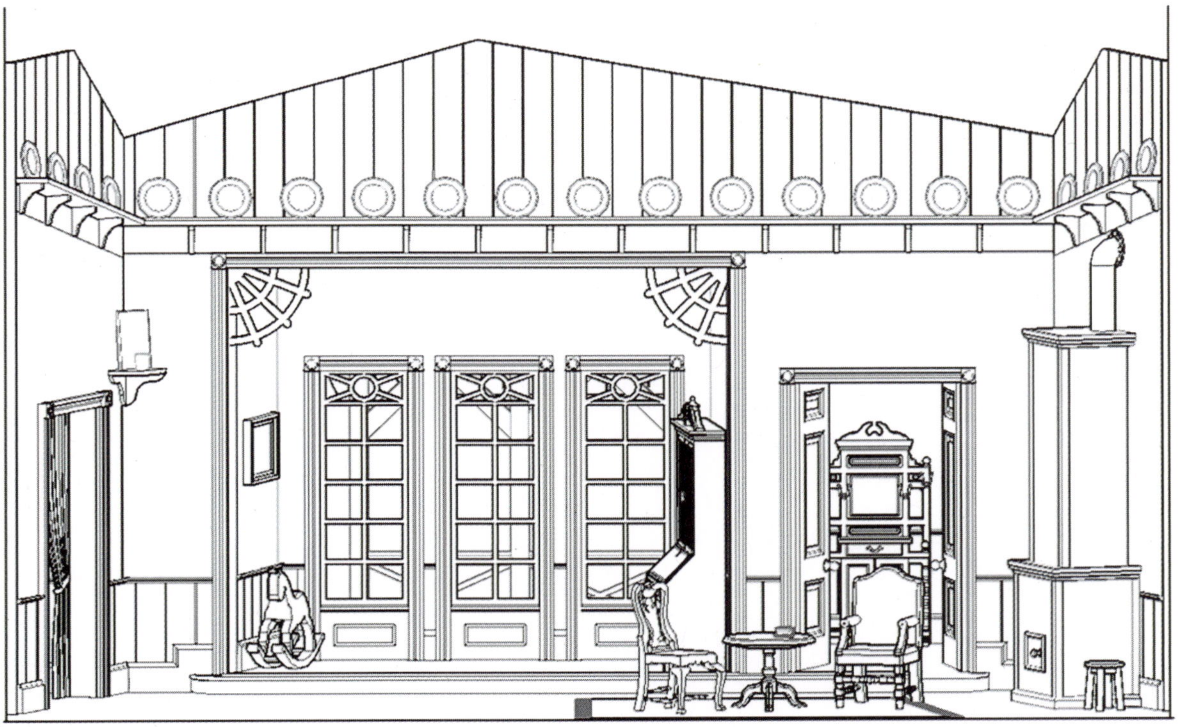

Outline rendering of a set for Act I of *The Cherry Orchard.*

Final rendering with images, patterns, textures and atmospheric lighting applied.

taken from the library of textures that came with the CAD software – in this case, *AutoCAD*.

The lighting in a digital model can give some impression of the effect to be created on stage, but as the digital light sources are so very different from those that will be used in reality, it offers little practical help when designing the real rig and lighting plot. Several attempts have been made to design a program that can do this, but most of them have achieved little general success. A dedicated lighting design program called *WYSIWYG* ('What You See Is What You Get'-https://cast-soft.com/wysiwyg-lighting-design) is the most popular of these, but seems to be aimed primarily at large-scale productions such as pop concerts, involving huge rigs of spectacular lighting and special effects. It is an impressive program with a great many features, but although it is possible to use it for less lavish productions in smaller venues, it is not generally used for this kind of show.

WALK-THROUGHS AND FLY-THROUGHS

A walk-through video of a fully modelled digital stage set not only looks impressive, but also has a useful practical function in showing what the set will look like when viewed from various parts of the auditorium. The illustration [below] shows a sequence of stills from a walk-through video created from the digital model of the set for *Shakespeare's Dog* described in Chapter 2.

There is a balance to be struck here, because a single hi-res rendering can take a long time to process, and a large number of such images is needed to create really smooth movement in a video sequence. The video illustrated here lasts for 18.5sec, contains a total of 52 frames, and took several hours to produce on a computer with a reasonably fast graphics processor. Fewer frames may be used, but this will inevitably result in a jerky movement. It is also possible to save processing time by using smaller images, but this would mean a loss of detail and a less impressive video. Fortunately the program can safely be left to work overnight, and then with luck, the completed video can be viewed for the first time over a morning coffee.

The first step in creating a walk- or fly-through is to designate a path for the digital camera to move along. The track can be straight or curved, but for continuous movement a circular or elliptical track is required so that at the last frame, the camera has returned to a position immediately before its start, ready to set off again without an obvious break. The drawing at right shows the camera track for the *Shakespeare's Dog* walk-through.

The track here is set approximately at a seated eye level and tilts with the slope of the stepped auditorium. Other details to be specified are the camera's 'target' (the centre of the stage in this case), and the size and number of frames. Most programs offer the user the opportunity to view a rapidly produced, very low-resolution run-through when setting these parameters, so final adjustments can be made before committing to the lengthy process of rendering the final hi-res version.

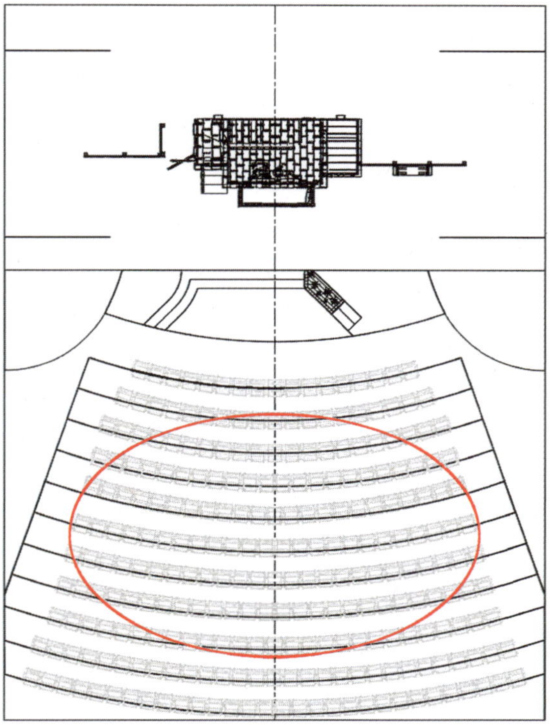

Top view of the digital auditorium and stage showing the camera track.

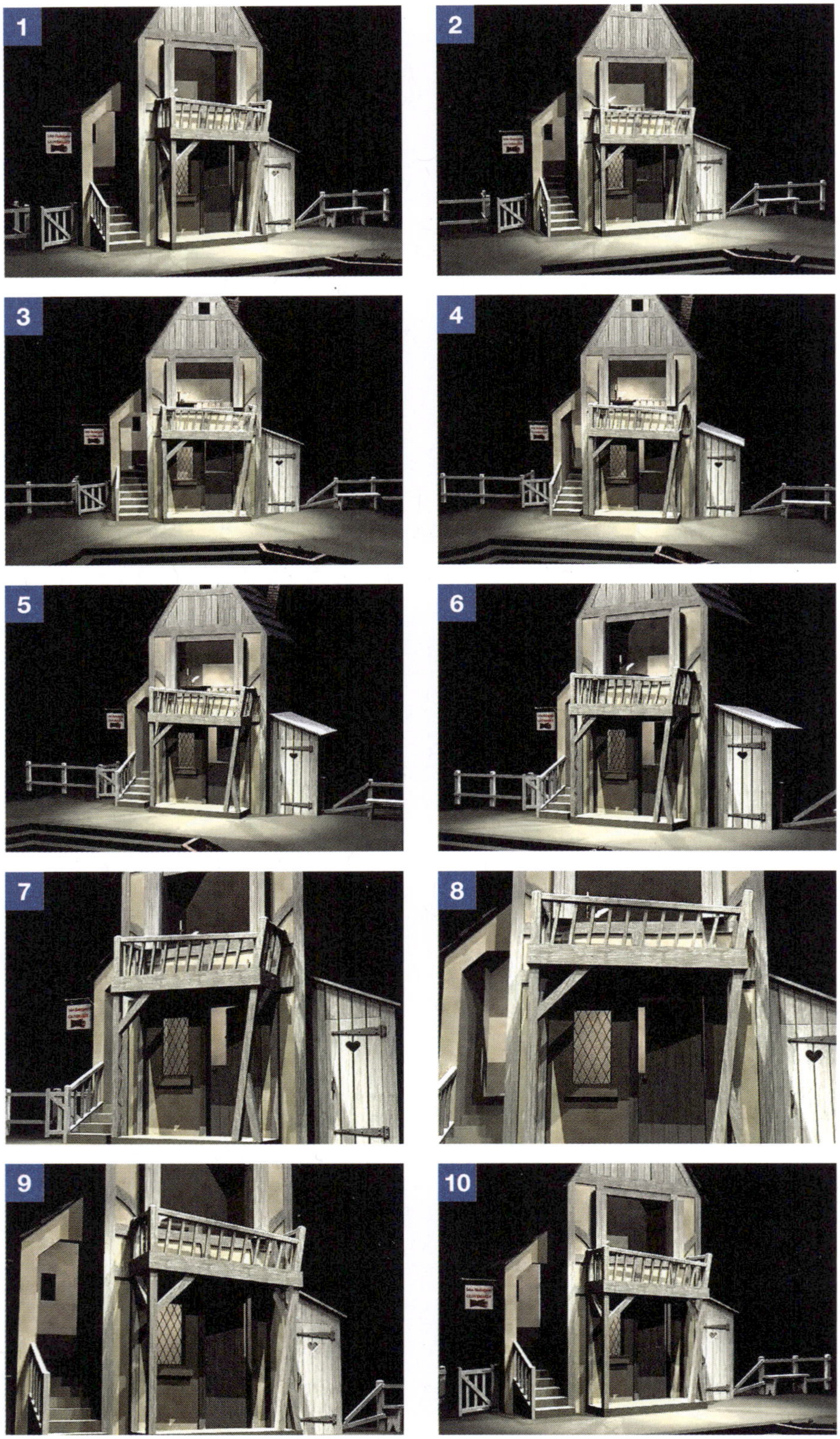

Frames from a walk-through video of a digital model.

A Schools Tour

The renderings below show a small fit-up set designed for *Opera della Luna*, a celebrated company of actor-singers, to tour a traditional pantomime around schools. The 'toy theatre'-inspired stage is intended to be set up in venues such as a school assembly hall or gym, so the digital model is designed to show it installed in a prototypical school hall. The entire room has been modelled, including the temporary seating, all four walls and ceiling. As some views from behind the set looking out towards the auditorium are intended to be rendered, structural details of the set that are normally hidden have also been included.

The fly-through shows the set from all round the audience seating area, but in this case, the digital camera travels up the steps on to the assembly-hall stage and moves round the back of the set in continuous motion.

CGI of a touring pantomime set on a school stage.

Frames from a fly-through video of the school hall and stage.

4
3D PRINTERS

3D printing, sometimes called 'rapid prototyping' or 'additive manufacturing', was developed during the 1980s and 1990s, but the machines were extremely expensive and consequently were found only in well-funded manufacturing and research establishments. However, by 2000, although they were still expensive, the cost had fallen sufficiently for 3D printers to be used industrially for the construction of architectural models and the like. They were also used in hospitals to produce three-dimensional models from a patient's CT or MRI scan to help with the examination of some pathological conditions. The idea that within just a few years low-cost desktop versions would be available for theatre designers to use in their home studios seemed pure fantasy at that time.

Early 3D printers such as the Z-Corp Z400 used the MJF or 'multi-jet fusion' method: a thin layer of a finely powdered plaster was laid down on the base plate, and an ink-jet printer head, guided by an adjacent computer, moved over the layer of powder printing, not with ink, but with a special binding liquid that hardened the powdered plaster wherever it came into contact with it. When the first layer had been printed, the plate was lowered slightly, and the process repeated until the whole object had been built up layer by layer. The large amount of unhardened powder remaining fell into a bin below to be recycled.

The object was then moved to a sealed cabinet (second from the right in the photograph overleaf) and blasted with an air gun to remove any remaining powder. Finally it was placed in another cabinet (extreme right in the photograph) to be coated with a layer of wax, which sealed the surface and provided some extra strength. The result was an accurate model but still rather fragile, and due to the wax surface, resistant to water-bound paints. The same basic method, though greatly improved, is still used by some commercial 3D printers today.

On discovering a 3D printer, possibly on a university campus, theatre designers immediately recognised its potential as an aid in the construction of set models – always the most time-consuming part of the entire design process. The photograph on the opposite page shows a 3D printed model made in 2001 of the set for Mozart's opera *Don Giovanni* produced by Opera Nuova. It is fully modelled, including some of the backstage elements such as masking and get-off steps, and is probably the first set model ever produced on a 3D printer. However, this was really not the best use of the technology, for although the model was printed at the maximum size possible on the Z-Corp Z400, it measured less than 30cm across, which is far too small for an effective set presentation to a roomful of opera singers or stage technicians.

Photograph and 3D printed model of the set for Opera Nuova's production of *Don Giovanni.*

Its fragility was also a problem, and it proved impossible to paint because apart from the wax-coated rough-textured surface that resisted water-colour, some parts were completely inaccessible to a paintbrush. Consequently, a hand-made model at a scale of 1:25 and built from wood and card in the traditional way was still required, and the 3D printed model, although it caused some excitement, served no practical function and lengthened the overall design process instead of shortening it. More practical uses for 3D printing in the construction of set models are discussed in Chapter 5.

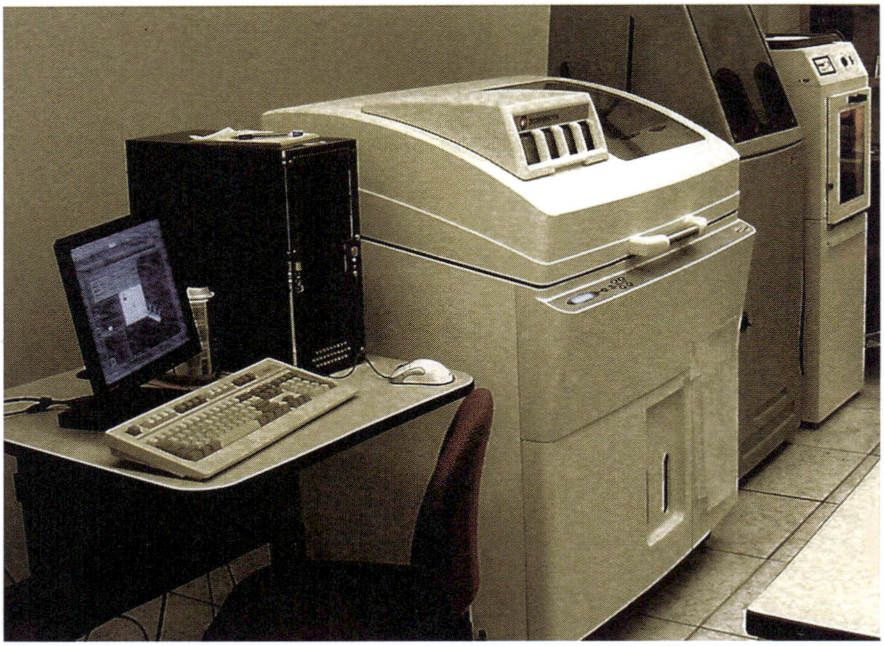

The Z-Corp Z400 3D printer.

Rear view of a 3D-printed set model for *Don Giovanni*.

3D PRINTING METHODS

Fused Deposition Modelling (FDM)

FDM is the technique used by most desktop 3D printers. It refers to the process of creating objects by fusing together very thin layers of plastic as they are laid down by the printer. To do this, the digital object first has to be horizontally 'sliced' into layers by the printer's software. The thermoplastic filament is then drawn from its coil and passed through a heated nozzle that moves over the printer's base-plate or 'platen', extruding a fine thread of the molten plastic to define each consecutive layer, which then fuses to the layer beneath it, gradually building up the whole object.

The thickness of the extruded filament can be controlled by the user, thus defining the height of each layer. Thinner layers give a better result, but extend the printing time. Any sizeable solid areas are created by filling an outer 'shell' with a honeycomb-type mesh instead of solid plastic, thereby saving a considerable amount of filament. The thickness of the shell and percentage of 'fill' are also controllable by the user.

Types of Filament

Many types of filament are available for use in 3D printers, but to a large extent the type used will depend upon the printer. Most frequently encountered are ABS (acetonitrile butadiene styrene) and PLA (polylactic acid). ABS is the stronger of the two, but has some serious disadvantages: it is not biodegradable, it requires a very high printing temperature, and gives off noxious fumes when in use, making a well-ventilated work space essential. PLA, on the other hand, is 100 per cent biodegradable and prints at a somewhat lower temperature, which makes it by far the more popular choice for home use. Most filaments are 'hygroscopic', which means they easily absorb moisture from the atmosphere, so to prevent degradation, when not in use they should be stored with the little packet of silica gel in the resealable plastic bag they came in.

Another type of filament to be considered is PETG (polyethylene terephthalate glycol). Objects created with it are very strong, but flexible, with a much smoother finish than PLA or ABS. It is easily biodegradable and prints without odour, but in spite of these advantages, many 3D printers cannot accept it, and PLA remains the most popular filament for its ease of use and lower cost.

Whichever type of filament is selected, there is a wide range of colours to choose from. Some are translucent, sparkly or fluorescent; others are designed to imitate materials such as wood, marble or metal, many of which contain the actual material in a finely powdered form. However, theatre designers printing parts for set models and intending to apply a paint finish will probably find a basic white or off-white the most convenient colours.

Resin-Based 3D Printing

A resin-based 3D printer uses a completely different technology: instead of filament, it uses a photosensitive liquid resin that solidifies when exposed to UV light. Objects are printed either 'bottom up' or 'top down,' (*see* overleaf) the major differences being the position of the UV light source and the direction the print-bed travels when printing. Most printers use the 'bottom-up' method with the liquid resin at the bottom, so objects are printed upside down. This is perfect for small-sized objects such as those intended for use in set models, but for larger objects there are weight limitations.

The digital model first has to be 'sliced' by the preparation software as in a filament-based process, but the layers are typically much thinner than those used in FDM printers, typically around 35 to 50µm (micrometres or microns) – the equivalent of 0.035 to 0.05mm.

The 'resin vat' is filled with liquid resin and UV light is filtered through an LCD screen with an image of the layer to be printed. This permits the light to pass only through the image area to harden that part of the resin. The platen is then moved by the thickness of a single layer and the process is

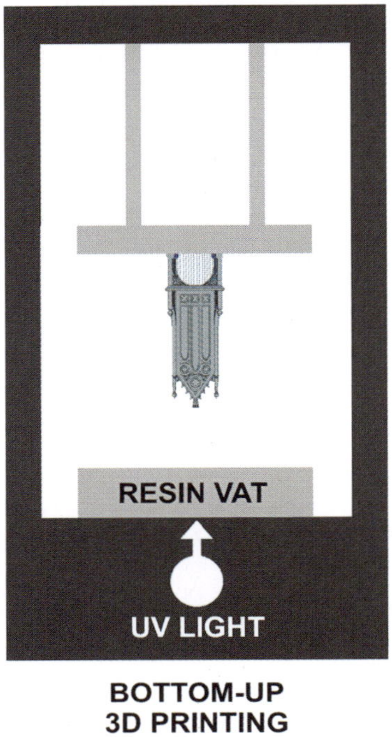

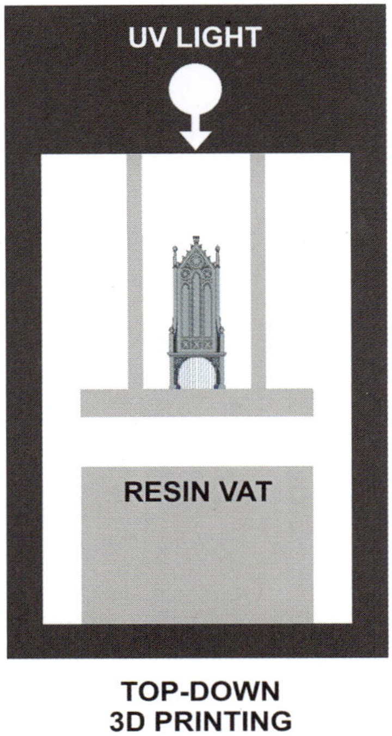

'Bottom-up' and 'top-down' resin-based 3D printing.

1:25-scale throne model from a resin-based printer.

repeated until the whole object has been built up layer by layer.

When the completed model is removed from the vat it must be washed to remove the surplus resin. To do this, many resins require isopropyl alcohol (IPA) or 'rubbing alcohol', but water-washable resins are also available that are easier to use. With these, rinsing in warm water will also release most of the thin supports that are added during printing, though a craft knife may be needed for larger or more stubborn supports. There will inevitably be some uncured resin remaining in the wash water, which should be removed by solidifying it with UV light before disposing of the polluted water, thereby avoiding any possible negative environmental and health impact when it gets mixed with groundwater. Finally, the completed model is exposed to UV light once again for final hardening.

The post-processing required by resin-based printers is somewhat complicated and messy, but the result is usually a stronger, smoother and more finely detailed model than is possible with filament-based printers.

Safety Precautions

* 3D printers should be used only in a well-ventilated area, and never left to run unsupervised.
* Some parts of filament-based printers become very hot when in use, so make sure that fingers (especially children's fingers) are kept well away when printing is in progress.
* The fumes from melted ABS filament are toxic, so a face mask is recommended when in use.
* Remember that ABS is a petroleum-based plastic that can easily catch fire. Keep it well away from heat or open flames.

For Resin-Based Printers:

* Plastic resin is a toxic material that should not be inhaled or come into contact with the skin, so wear gloves and a face mask when using it, and always handle it with great care. If you get any on your skin, wash it off immediately with soap and water.
* To avoid overflow, take care not to fill the resin vat beyond the MAX line, and use it on a surface that is easy to clean in the event of a spill. A large protective silicone mat (available from Amazon) is recommended when working with partially cured prints.
* Always clean the resin vat and platen after use to prevent accumulation of cured resin particles.
* Liquid resin should be stored in an opaque bottle with a tight lid to avoid exposure to sunlight and heat.
* Isopropyl alcohol is flammable, so always keep it well away from heat or open flames.

Which Printer?

Selecting the 3D printer that is best for your own particular requirements can be perplexing. Here are some considerations to bear in mind:

* Price: All models will produce effective 3D prints, but the more expensive ones come with extra features and are generally more user-friendly in operation.
* Build size: This varies considerably – mid-range desktop printers are usually capable of printing up to about 25 × 25 × 25cm, but some of the cheaper models have a much smaller platen.
* Many printers require some degree of 'self-assembly', while other models can be used 'straight out of the box'. Unsurprisingly, the fully assembled models tend to be more expensive.
* Some models are completely open on all sides and others are contained within a closed box structure. As 3D printers contain moving parts that become very hot when in use, this may be an important consideration if young children have access to your work space. Closed-box printers are also quieter in operation, but generally more expensive than the open-sided type.
* What type of filament does the printer use? Usually PLA – but there are other possibilities (*see* above).
* A resin-based printer: this is trickier and rather messy to use, but it produces excellent results.

Some Popular 3D Printers

Below is an annotated list of some of the most popular 3D printers at the time of writing, which may help in deciding which features you might want to prioritise.

Creality Ender – 3 V3
(https://www.creality.com)

Open-sided, and requires some self-assembly. A best-seller for many years, possibly because of its low price. It works best with PLA filament, but will also accept ABS and PETG. It is easy to operate, but noisy when printing. The platen sometimes needs to be treated with a glue stick (included) to increase adhesion. Build size: 22 × 22 × 25cm.

Original Prusa i3 Mk 3S
(https://www.prusa3D.com)

Open-sided, available in assembled or self-assembly versions. It accepts PLA and PETG filaments, with a built-in filament sensor that can detect the type and colour of filament in use. A two-spool filament holder makes it capable of switching colours during printing. A 'pause' feature enables it to continue printing from exactly where it left off. Build size: 21 × 21 × 25cm.

Creality Ender – 3 V3.

MakerBot Replicator+
(https://www.makerbot.com)

Partly enclosed in a sturdy steel frame. It comes fully assembled and ready for use straight out of the box. It uses PLA filament only. A removable, flexible platen makes the removal of strongly adhered completed prints much easier. The 'pause' feature

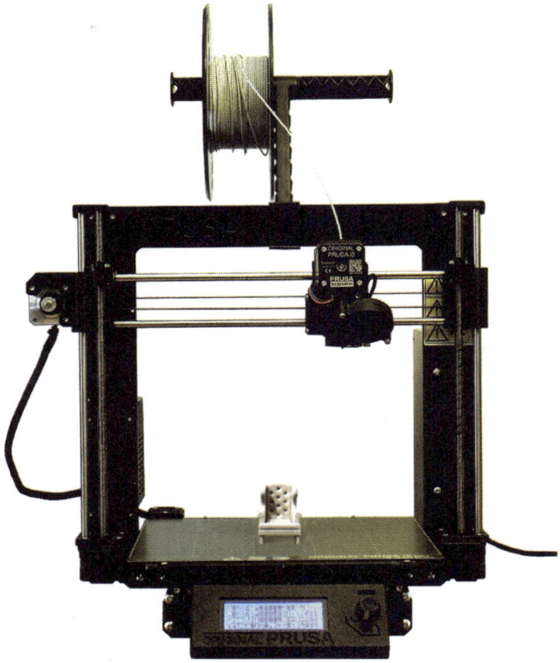

Original Prusa i3 Mk 3S.

MakerBot Replicator+.

enables it to continue printing from exactly where it left off. It contains a camera in the print head for remote monitoring. Build size: 19.5 × 16.5 × 29.5cm.

Elegoo Saturn 4 Ultra

(https://www.elegoo.com)

This is a resin-based printer. It comes fully assembled, and is completely enclosed when in use. It produces strong, smooth, finely detailed models that require some inconvenient and rather messy post-processing. There is a built-in AI camera for remote monitoring. Build size: 21.9 × 12.3 × 22cm.

Bambu Lab P1S

(https://www.bambulab.com)

Fully enclosed, and no assembly is required, but there is a prescribed 'unboxing' process. It accepts PLA, ABS and PETG filaments. This is a multicolour printer that can hold four reels of filament in different colours, and can be expanded up to sixteen colours by connecting the Bambu Lab Automatic Material System (AMS) – this is available for purchase. The colour painting tool in Bambu Studio (https://bambulab.com/en/download/studio) enables the user to preselect which parts of the object will be printed in each colour. The 'pause' feature enables it to continue printing from exactly where it left off. There is a built-in camera for remote monitoring, and a useful selection of maintenance tools and spare parts is included. Build size: 25.6 × 25.6 × 25.6cm.

Elegoo Saturn 4 Ultra.

Bambu Lab P1S.

PREPARING TO PRINT

Most 3D printers come with their own dedicated software for converting the STL files exported from a 3D modelling program to a format that can be understood by that particular printer. Usually this not only slices the digital objects to the desired layer thickness, but also controls many other features such as the thickness of the 'shell' and the percentage of honeycomb 'fill'. The overall size of the object to be printed can also be adjusted here, and if several items are to be printed at the same time, the software will automatically position them on the platen in an arrangement suitable for printing. The illustration shows a screen-grab from the *MakerBot Print* software when preparing to print furniture parts for the set model of *The Government Inspector* described in Chapter 3.

Several free, open-source slicer programs are available online, the most popular of which is *Cura* (https://ultimaker.com/software/ultimaker-cura) developed by *UltiMaker,* the Dutch 3D printer manufacturer. It is user-friendly and contains all the features you could ever need.

A popular slicer for resin-based 3D printers is *Chitubox* (https://www.chitubox.com/en/download/chitubox-free). The basic version, which is compatible with most resin printers, is free to download and has a user-friendly interface that will also orientate objects for printing and generate any necessary supports.

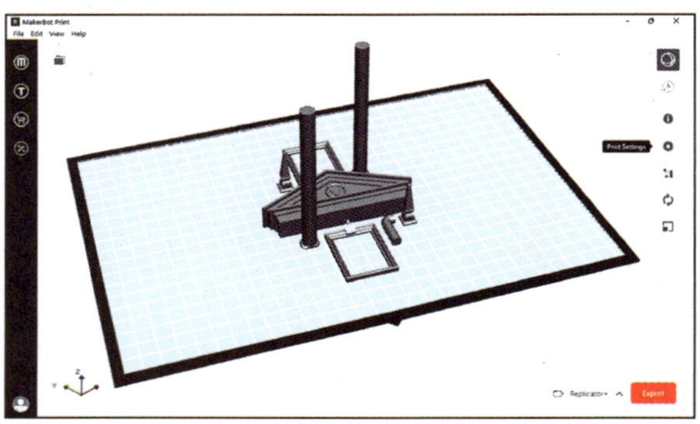

The *MakerBot Print* screen showing the automatic arrangement of model parts.

To prevent warping, objects must adhere firmly to the platen during printing. To provide extra adherence, most pre-print programs can enable the use of a 'raft'. This consists of a few loosely constructed layers of plastic, slightly larger than the object's footprint, that are laid on to the platen before beginning the actual build. A raft is especially effective when the object has a large base area, but the increased adherence can sometimes make it difficult to remove, and it is easy to snap off some of the finer details in the process. Some 3D printers, such as the *MakerBot* range, have an easily removable, flexible platen that is a great help here – but slipping a painter's palette knife or scraper underneath the raft will usually solve the problem, so it is a good idea to keep two or three palette knives of varying sizes beside the printer. Once removed from the platen, the raft can be peeled off the printed object with the aid of pliers if necessary.

Dealing with Overhangs

A frequently recurring problem with FDM, or filament-based 3D printing, is coping with unsupported or overhanging areas. Thus when printing, say, a model table, the printer begins printing at the bottom of each leg, building up all four legs in consecutive layers until it reaches

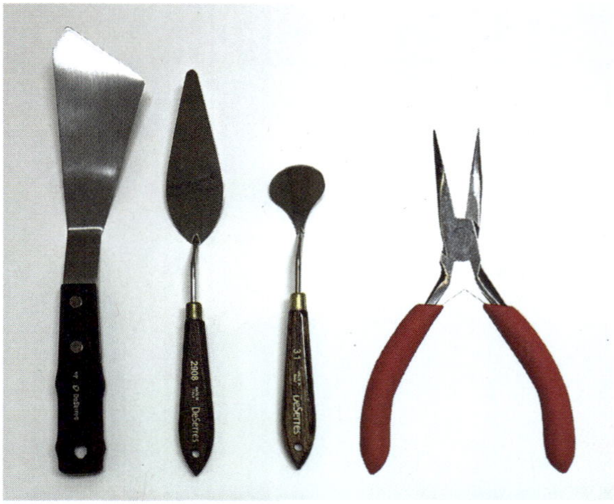

A selection of removal tools.

the table top. But to create the table top the extruded filament needs to cross from the top of each leg to the top of the next. However, it cannot do this as there is nothing to support it, so the filament drops and ends up in a tangled mess on the platen.

With an item such as a table, the problem can often be overcome by simply printing it upside down, but more complicated overhangs require more drastic solutions, and most pre-print programs offer the use of 'supports' as a bridging technique. When these are enabled, the printer automatically constructs thin columns of filament beneath any unsupported areas. Some supports are designed to be 'breakaway' and can easily be snapped off, but others are sturdier and have to be removed with pliers and a craft knife, so there is a danger that some of the finer details may be damaged in the process.

The overhang problem can be avoided altogether with some careful advance planning. Chair legs, for example, may be printed separately and glued in place after printing. This has an added advantage that each part can be sanded and painted before final assembly, making the process much easier and less liable to cause breakages. When designing model parts to be assembled after printing, it is helpful to create a small peg on one of the contact surfaces, and provide a slot in the corresponding piece for the peg to fit into. This ensures that each part is positioned precisely as intended. The grand piano in the illustration shows an example of this technique: it is printed in seven parts, and each part has a peg that fits into a slot in the adjacent part. Note that the slots need to be a little bigger than the pegs – about 0.2mm all round for a snug fit.

To fix the plastic parts permanently into position a superglue containing cyanoacrylate is required. The kind that comes in gel form is more controllable than the liquid type, with the added advantage that it takes a little longer to 'grab', so there is time to reposition the part before it sets if this is needed. Do not try to use the gel directly out of the tube, but squeeze a few drops on to a piece of waste card, then you can apply a tiny amount just where it is needed with a toothpick or cocktail stick.

Cyanoacrylate is a toxic substance and should always be used in a well-ventilated area. Bear in mind that it was originally developed as an adhesive for human flesh, and as it is almost inevitable that some will get on to your fingers when working with it, you should always keep some solvent handy. (In an emergency, nail varnish remover is an effective solvent.) If cyanoacrylate gets into the eyes it can cause serious injuries, so if this should happen, it is crucial to rinse them with lukewarm water for fifteen minutes before seeking urgent medical attention.

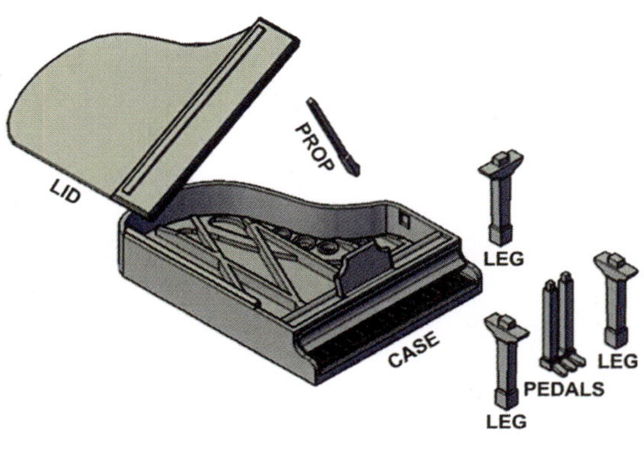

Parts for a 3D printed grand piano model.

The grand piano model assembled.

FINISHING AND PAINTING

After the object has been removed from the platen and raft, a little cleaning up is usually required to remove any stray threads of filament and smooth the slightly striated surface. A craft knife and some manicurist's tools such as a nail file and emery board are helpful here. This may seem a somewhat tedious task, but when printing parts for a finely detailed set model, it is time well spent.

An undercoat of artist's gesso will provide a smooth, stone-like finish to 3D printed objects with a good surface for matt painting if this is required, but for most general purposes, a coat of white or off-white artist's acrylic paint, applied straight out of the tube with as little water added as possible, will provide a reasonable undercoat for gouache or watercolour.

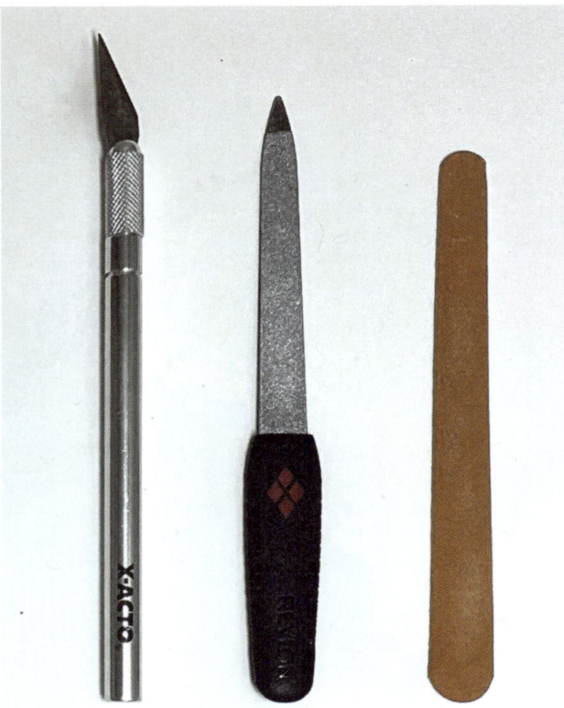

Finishing tools.

Objects that will be frequently handled, such as the scale furniture in set models, can be finished with a coat of matt artist's varnish for protection, or apply one or two coats of gloss varnish to give a shine to surfaces representing materials such as polished wood, metal or marble. Spirit-bound varnishes, such as those intended for use on oil paintings, work best (in spite of the 'not suitable for watercolour' warning on the bottle), because acrylic varnishes, although easier to apply, have a tendency to pick up the water-based paints beneath them and cause smudging.

3D PRINTING IN COLOUR

Popular types of filament are available in a wide range of colours. Some printers, such as the *Bambu Lab P1S*, can hold several reels of different coloured filaments at the same time, which they can use in pre-programmed areas to produce multicoloured objects – but in the forefront of 3D printing are 'full colour' printers.

These are large machines that use a colourless filament that is surface-dyed during the printing process with the same kind of CMYK coloured inks used by 2D printers. The results are startlingly effective, but at the time of writing, full-colour 3D printers are extremely expensive and far beyond the budget of most stage designers. However, when the first coloured 2D printers came on the market many years ago, they too were very expensive machines, but they rapidly plummeted in price until now they often cost less than a set of replacement ink cartridges – so it's quite possible that full-colour 3D printers may develop in the same way, and by the time you are reading this book they could be commonplace in our studios. This would mean that subtly coloured digital models may be converted to identically coloured physical models by our 3D printers without the intervention of a paintbrush.

LARGE-SCALE 3D PRINTING

Full-sized residential houses are now being constructed using liquid concrete extruded from machines that work as large-scale 3D printers. The logical consequence of this is that theatre workshops will soon be able to use a similar technique to produce full-sized stage sets directly from the digital models created by the designer, and with the help of advanced colour-printing techniques, in full colour too.

On the other hand, theatre, in all its aspects, is essentially a collaborative art form, and the experience and technical know-how of our theatre carpenters, props makers and scene painters are invaluable assets that cannot be replaced by technology. A stage designer's work is inevitably enhanced when it is developed by an experienced and co-operative team of workshop technicians, and a careful comparison of the four photographs that form the frontispiece to this book will show that the set that actually appeared on stage had an engaging human quality that is not apparent in the digital version.

Full colour 3D printer by *Mimaki.*

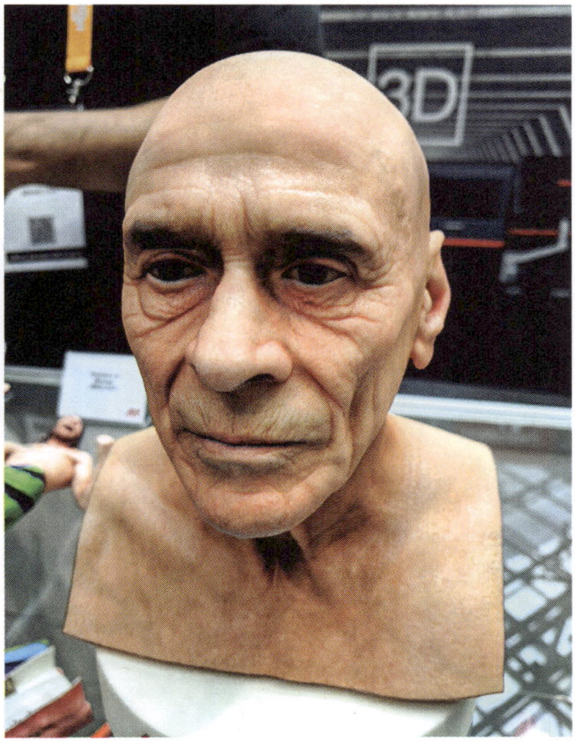

Full colour 3D printed mask.

5
3D PRINTING FOR SET MODELS

Working in any aspect of theatre involves a strict adherence to deadlines. For the production team, the most significant deadlines are first rehearsal and opening night, but the designer's deadlines for delivery of set and costume designs are put at a much earlier stage in the process, as practical work on a production cannot begin without them. For this reason, designers need to schedule their work with care to be sure it can be completed in the time available. The most time-consuming part of the entire design process is usually the construction of the set model, which always seems to take

Set model for *The Government Inspector.*

2D and 3D printed parts for a physical set model.

much longer than anticipated, so having carefully estimated how long a model will take to build, a wise designer will allow at least *twice* that length of time to be safe.

It has already been pointed out that printing a complete set model on a 3D printer is not a practical proposition, for not only are the traditional materials such as cardboard and wood more suitable for making most of the parts, but they also provide much more sympathetic surfaces for painting in watercolour. However, there are many ways in which the shrewd use of a 3D printer can considerably shorten the length of time spent on model building.

The illustration on page 73 shows the 1:25-scale set model for the production of Gogol's *The Government Inspector* referred to earlier. All the furniture pieces were made on a 3D printer, but the only 3D printed parts of the actual set are shown in the photograph below. These are all parts that can be more efficiently produced by a 3D printer than by hand. (The columns might have been made from lengths of dowel, but in this case the back of each column was slightly flattened to fit flush to the wall behind.)

The wallpaper pattern, stove tiles and oil paintings that had already been designed at full size for the CGI set renderings, were reduced to scale and printed on to paper with a desktop ink-jet printer. They were then glued to the mountboard walls with a spray adhesive. (Sprayed adhesives are somewhat inconvenient as they are imprecise and need to be used in a protected, well-ventilated area, rather than the intimate space of the average designer's studio, but the type of glue generally used for making models, such as PVA or 'white glue', produces irremovable wrinkles when used for gluing paper to a flat surface and needs to be avoided.)

3D printed parts for the set model.

SCALE FURNITURE

Building the furniture for set models is usually the most time-consuming part of the entire process, and it is here that a 3D printer can be particularly useful. The 1:25 scale, entirely hand-made player-piano on the left in the photograph below took a day to make from scratch, whereas the piano on the right took just over an hour to design in 3D *AutoCAD*, complete with piano stool, and less than an hour to produce on a 3D printer while work on other parts of the model continued, and is now ready for painting.

Having designed a piece of digital furniture, the DWG and STL files should be saved to an appropriately named file for future use. In this way a designer can gradually build up a sizeable collection, and future set models may need only one or two specially designed items of furniture, supplemented by other pieces drawn from the digital store, thereby saving a large amount of valuable model-making time.

The furniture in the *Government Inspector* set model consists of a large dining table, four upright chairs, one chair with arms, one small side chair, and a couch. The only piece of furniture that had to be digitised especially for this model was the couch – all the rest had been created for previous projects and the files stored. Most of the items are designed to be printed in several parts, making a total of 28 parts in all. They were all printed at the same time, which took a little over three hours, but while they were being printed work continued on the rest of the model.

A Digital Props Store

A comparison of the furniture in the photograph of the model on page 73 with the furniture as it actually appeared on stage in the photograph on page 45 shows hardly any discernible difference. This is because the furniture was selected from the theatre's props store at an early stage in the design process. Several of the pieces had already been digitised, but new pieces were measured,

Handmade model piano (left) and 3D printed model piano (right).

MakerBot Print screen showing the arrangement of furniture pieces on the platen ready for printing.

The assembled 3D printed furniture ready to be painted.

photographed and recreated in 3D *AutoCAD* to form part of the digital set model for CGI rendering, and later printed out to scale on a 3D printer for inclusion in the physical model.

In an ideal world, a theatre's props department would have digital models of all the pieces of furniture in its store freely available online in DWG and STL formats. This would save much time and effort for both designers and props supervisors, because the designers would be able to search through the store from their home studios, without having to make an appointment with the supervisor to climb over dusty sofas, measuring tape in hand, in an attempt to examine a particular chair tucked away at the back – and, of course, the digital versions of the pieces selected could be downloaded and used as described above.

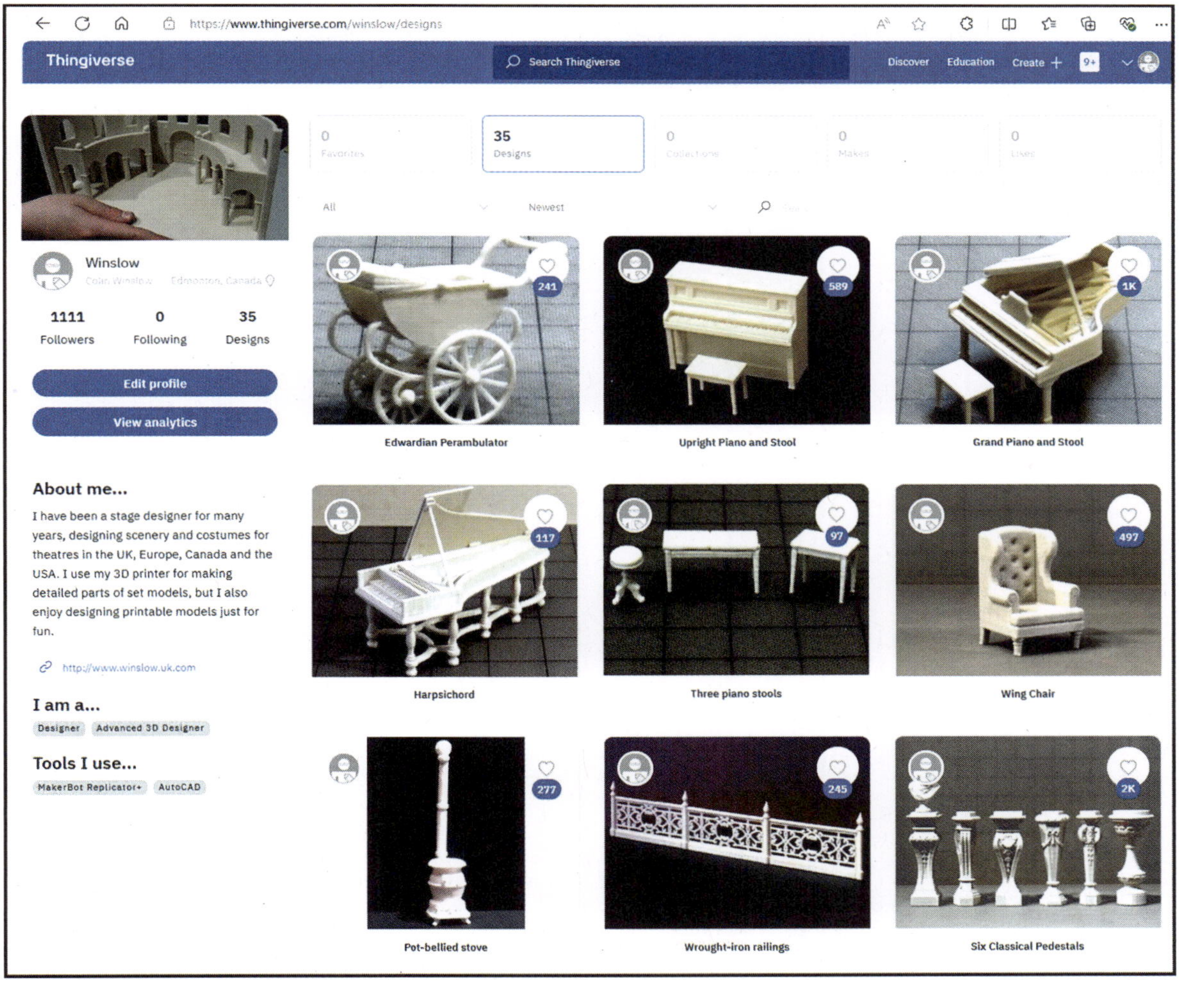

The author's *Thingiverse* page.

3D MODELS FOR FREE!

For designers who have access to a 3D printer but do not relish the task of creating their own models, there are many internet sites that offer digital models in STL format to be downloaded for 3D printing – some of which are entirely free. One of the most popular of these sites is *The Thingiverse* (https://www.thingiverse.com), which contains literally thousands of freely downloadable STL files for a wide variety of objects. Unfortunately, some of them, although enthusiastically designed, are not actually printable, so look for those entries that show photographs of the printed objects and not just the digital renderings, and check the number of times they have been printed by other users.

Many of the items to be found in *The Thingiverse* are of particular interest to theatre designers: set designer Kacie Hultgren (https://www.kaciehultgren.com), for instance, under the username 'prettysmallthings', has many useful items, including some well-designed pieces of furniture, and Ronn Campbell, Associate Professor of Theatre at Columbia Basin College in Washington, under the username 'Ronnskull', has a good selection of theatrical items such as lighting and sound equipment, trusses, auditorium seating and so on. All of them print well, and although most are at scale 1:24 (1/2in to 1ft) or 1:12 (1in to 1ft – dolls' house scale) the slight adjustment required to convert them to 1:25 can easily be made when preparing to print.

The author's own *Thingiverse* pages (https://www.thingiverse.com/winslow/designs) contain several of the furniture pieces referred to in this book (*see* previous page).

CHANGING THE SCALE

Although the recommended scale for set models is 1:25, there are some occasions, particularly when designing for a very large stage, when a 1:50-scale

Hospital bed printed at scale 1:50.

3D print enlarged from a miniature version.

Commercially printed model furniture.

model is more convenient. Many designers will have already discovered that making accurate model furniture by hand at a small scale such as 1:50 is a much more onerous and time-consuming task than when working at the larger scale. However, when preparing a model for 3D printing, the size can easily be changed with the preparation software, so it should be possible to reduce the scale of a printed object from 1:25 to 1:50 with just a couple of but unfortunately this rarely results in a successful print, as thin parts, such as chair legs, usually turn out to be too thin to print at the new scale, and even with the layers reduced to their minimum thickness, they turn out so fragile that they frequently break as they are being removed from the platen. So when printing at very small scales, it is usually preferable to redesign the pieces from scratch, thickening the thin parts and enlarging very small details to a printable size. The results may look a little clumsy, but at least they will be printable.

The actual size of the 1:50-scale hospital bed and rolling tray in the picture on page 78 is 3.75 × 2.00cm. However, this model required so many trials and tiny adjustments to make it printable that it would probably have been quicker to have made it by hand.

Printing objects at a scale *larger* than originally designed is generally more successful. Curved surfaces may appear slightly faceted if they are greatly enlarged, but these can be sanded down to a uniform smoothness when completed. The photograph at the top of page 79 shows a 3D print, straight off the platen, of a piece of period chinaware enlarged to full size from its original miniature version by the *MakerBot Print* software. If intended for use on stage, a piece of expensive-looking chinaware created in this way has the great advantage of being virtually unbreakable.

3D PRINTING WITHOUT A PRINTER

If you do not have access to a 3D printer, it is still possible to include 3D-printed items in your set models by using a commercial 3D printing service. If you don't have one locally, an internet search will turn up many of these sites, most of them offering prints by a variety of methods and in a wide range of materials. Model files in STL and other formats are easily uploaded to the website by the 'drag and drop' method, where they are automatically assessed, and the user is immediately informed if they are printable, together with suggestions for suitable materials and the price. Estimated delivery time is usually five to seven days, but some firms offer an express service at an additional cost.

Any 'overhang' issues are eliminated by the printing method, and the results are generally of a high quality, with a smooth finish and good detailing. The picture at the bottom of page 79 shows four items made for the set model for a production of *Peter Pan* printed by *i.materialise* (https://i.materialise.com).

A STEP FURTHER

Pat Darbasie's one-woman play *Ribbon* is set in a Canadian settler's log cabin, so naturally, the set required an old-fashioned pot-bellied stove. The stove was designed as a 3D model in *AutoCAD*, and printed out to scale on a 3D printer to be included in the set model. The STL file was later used by a CNC (computer numerical control) router to carve a full-size version in 25cm horizontal sections from high-density polystyrene. The sections were then assembled in the theatre's props department, sanded to a smooth finish and painted black. Finally, the stove was rubbed with graphite to produce an iron-like sheen. The illustrations below show the development of the stove from a digital model to the full-sized prop as it appeared on stage. The model stove is now downloadable from *The Thingiverse*, as can be seen in the screen grab on page 77.

Digital model.

3D print.

Set model.

Production photograph.

CNC digital router.

SEASON'S GREETINGS
from Colin Winslow
Shakespeare's Dog – Rick Chafe
13
From who? The bar hag at the Bear and Crown who fancies you so much?
small actors!
A job, Will.
To become laced mutto
wheelwright's boy!
What makes you too s
Just wait till the bab
go…
You got three b
… just till w
WILL:
ANNE:
WILL:

6
USING DIGITAL IMAGERY

We see thousands of images every day, more than at any other time in history, though most of them are on a screen of some kind, and the printed images we see are usually in some commercial context. Until the late twentieth century printing pictures in full colour was much more expensive than printing in one colour only, because first the colours in the picture had to be separated photographically into red, yellow, blue and black, then a separate printing block was made for each colour. This meant that at least four print-runs were required to produce a fully coloured image, and as each print-run incurred an additional cost, the number of colours used was often deliberately restricted.

Advertising material in particular often adopted a very limited colour range, so when, as frequently happened, the set designer was asked to design a poster or a programme cover for a show, the first question asked was usually 'How many colours can I have?' (The answer was usually 'One, plus black'.) Fortunately this question is now irrelevant, as modern printing techniques handle colour in a much more efficient way, and most designers have a desktop printer that will produce high-resolution images in full colour at very little cost. Consequently, much of a theatre's publicity material is now designed on an office computer, using a program such as *Photoshop,* to avoid the costly employment of a professional graphic designer.

HARD COPY

Theatre designers produce images of various kinds for every show they work on, most of which are technical drawings stored digitally in a CAD format – but often hard-copy versions of the designer's work are not only more convenient, but absolutely essential: technicians building a set in the workshop, for example, usually work with a sheet of dimensioned construction drawings beside them, and the stage management will need a hard-copy version of the stage plan when marking out a set on the rehearsal-room floor so they can scribble notes and dimensions on to it as required.

They will also need many smaller, page-sized plans of the acting area to be glued between the

Using 2D prints of CAD imagery for set rendering, greetings card and small-scale stage plans.

Colour Matching

Colour is notoriously difficult to quantify, and the names we use to refer to colours are extremely vague, so what one person visualises as 'rose red', for instance, may be quite different from the colour another person visualises. Colours also change depending on the method used to reproduce them. An image created on a computer's monitor screen will look quite different when it is printed to hard copy on a desktop printer, and will change again when the image is reproduced by other means. This is partly because the colours we see on our monitors are created by combining the colours of the light spectrum, so the primary colours are not red, yellow and blue, as with pigment, but red, green and blue (which is why this format is referred to as 'RGB').

Lighting designers are familiar with this anomaly, as lights in these colours can combine to produce white light. Moreover, when an image is reproduced as hard copy, transparent coloured inks are used, and colours are defined as combinations of cyan, magenta, yellow and black – referred to as 'CMYK'. (Black is indicated by 'K' for 'key' to avoid confusion with blue.) A further, lesser-known method of defining colours is by HTML (hypertext mark-up language), which contains a system of colour codes for use in website design. (An easy-to-use HTML colour coder is available at https://htmlcolorcodes.com)

When really accurate colour matching is essential, such as when designing a company logo or selecting an organisation's 'house' colour, the usual solution is to use the Pantone Matching System (PMS) (https://www.pantone.com). Pantone issues sets of swatches, so colours can be matched to a particular swatch colour, and the CMYK, RGB or HTML values read off from the back, thereby ensuring an accurate reproduction of the colour whenever or however it is used.

pages of the prompt script, on which to record the actors' moves during rehearsals. Small-scale prints of the stage plan and set rendering should also be circulated to the actors to keep with their scripts so they can plot their own moves and visualise them in the set when learning lines.

A 1:25-scale copy of the plan should be taped to a wall of the rehearsal room for general reference, and as some technical know-how is required to interpret a stage plan, a large-sized colour print of the CGI set rendering alongside it can help the actors and director to visualise the set as it will eventually appear on stage.

A Sketch Model

The most valuable tool for visualising a stage set is the scale model as it shows all aspects of the set in a form that anyone can easily understand; but unfortunately, a detailed and accurate model takes a long time to make, and cannot be started until technical drawings are available – which is usually fairly late in the design process. However, a rapidly constructed, disposable sketch model can be a useful aid to visualisation for both the designer and the director, and it is not difficult to make one from the stage plan and technical drawings, even when they are still in the process of development. Technical drawings in CAD are created at full size and converted to an appropriate scale only when hard-copy versions are printed. So if they are reduced to a very small scale, such as 1:50, most of the set parts will be small enough to be printed out on a desktop printer – though probably not all on the same sheet.

A practical way to do this is to load the working drawings and the stage plan into your CAD program, hide any unwanted layers such as text, dimension lines, borders and logos, and scale everything remaining to 1:50. Then create several rectangles at 210 × 297mm – the dimensions of an A4 sheet – and arrange the set parts and the central part of the stage plan on to these 'pages'. All the parts of the set in the example opposite fitted easily on to three A4 sheets. Each of these pages can then be printed on to cardstock and

Model parts printed from technical drawings.

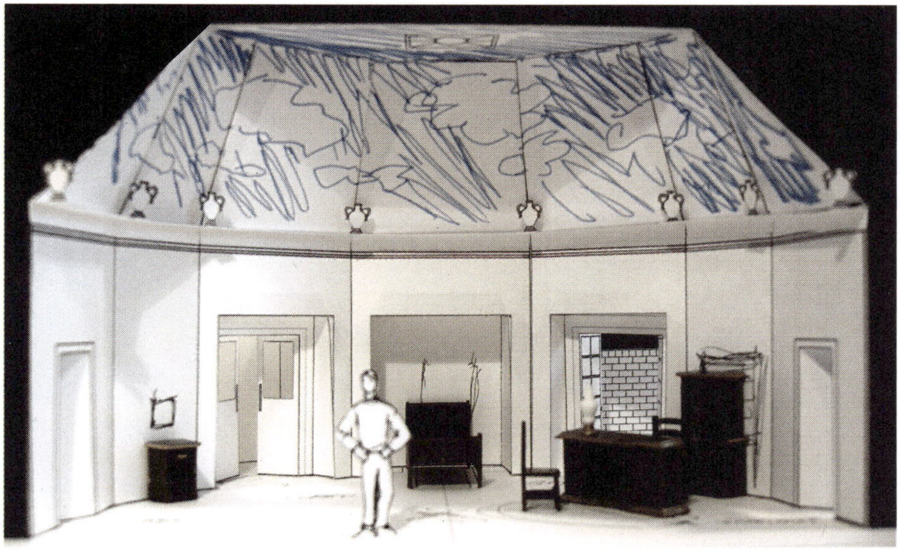

Small-scale sketch model.

the parts quickly cut out with scissors or a craft knife, and assembled on the plan, sticking them together with Sellotape.

The card model is now the three-dimensional equivalent of a rough sketch. Features such as set dressings and paint details can be scribbled on to it, and furniture arrangements can be tried out. The sketch model in the photograph was made for a production of Joe Orton's play *What the Butler Saw.* A painted cloud ceiling has been tentatively suggested with a felt-tip pen, which was eventually incorporated into the presentation model and the finished set. The furniture pieces, only a rough approximation of those that will appear on stage, are from a set of plastic 1:50-scale dolls' house furniture.

Greetings Cards

Theatre designers work in collaboration with many other people, including actors, technicians and other designers, but perhaps the closest and most significant collaboration is with the show's director, who usually chooses the designer he or she wishes to work with. For professional productions the designer will be contracted by the theatre's business manager or an independent production company, so theatre designers are always dependent on other theatre people for employment.

Some professional designers have an agent who will guide their career and help them to find work, but in the competitive world of theatre it can be advantageous for designers, whether professional or amateur, to undertake a little self-promotion from time to time. This may mean just keeping in touch by phone or email, or merely socialising, but as designers generally have some graphical skills, other possibilities are open to them: for instance, a computer-generated image of a recently designed set might be adapted for use as a greetings card, with the designer's name prominently displayed.

The pictures opposite show a digital rendering of the top part of the set for *Shakespeare's Dog*, but the lighting has been enhanced and some Christmas decorations have been added. With superimposed text, it was printed to cardstock and copies were mailed to the cast, the production team, the theatre management, and some directors worked with previously – primarily as a Christmas greetings card, but also to promote the designer's work. This kind of self-advertisement may seem a little crude, but providing it is not over-exploited, it can help to generate some future design work.

DESIGNING A WEBSITE

A big advantage that set and costume designers have over actors is that they can show pictures of their work to prospective employers. Actors can show photographs of how they appeared on stage, but these do not show how well they performed, whereas a photograph showing how the set and costumes appeared on stage gives a good impression of how well the designer has performed, so a website showing examples of the designer's work can be a valuable asset.

A theatre designer's website should not be viewed as part of social media. Its specific aim is to establish a professional reputation and generate work by demonstrating competence and artistic ability, and to do this it should offer answers to the kind of questions that might be asked at a face-to-face interview, such as: what design work have you done previously? Do you have a typical design style? Are you equally adept at designing both sets and costumes? Most of these questions can be answered by showing your CV and pictures of productions you have designed previously. Indicate the name of the show and the venue beside each picture, and also include the name of the director – not just as a

Computer-generated image with seasonal enhancements.

Text added for use as a greetings card.

courtesy, but as someone who may be contacted for a reference.

Showing some good press reviews can also be helpful, but keep any accompanying text as brief as possible: it is the pictures that will speak most about your work. The 'home page' – the page that appears first when a user logs on to your site – should be brief and to the point, with clear links to the other sections. The *Studio Secrets* book on web design (*see* Bibliography) suggests that a visitor should be able to navigate to any part of a website within three clicks or fewer.

Make sure that your contact details (email and/or phone number) are clearly displayed on the home page. You may not wish to disclose your address, but it's helpful to give some indication of where you are based.

To make your website active, you will need to employ a web-hosting service. A great many of these are to be found online, but a well-established site with a good reputation will offer a useful range of additional services such as domain name selection and registration, tools and templates for building your site, and one or more email addresses. Probably the most popular web-hosting service worldwide is *GoDaddy* at https://www.godaddy.com

FAVICONS

A favicon is a small icon that is automatically displayed beside the URL in a browser's address bar or linked to the name of the site wherever it may be listed. The standard size is only 16 × 16 pixels so the design needs to be kept very simple, but it can add a little distinction to your website and make it immediately recognisable. An online search will turn up many 'Favicon Design' sites, but a personal favourite is one from *Dan's Tools* (*see* Useful websites) at https://www.favicon-generator.org

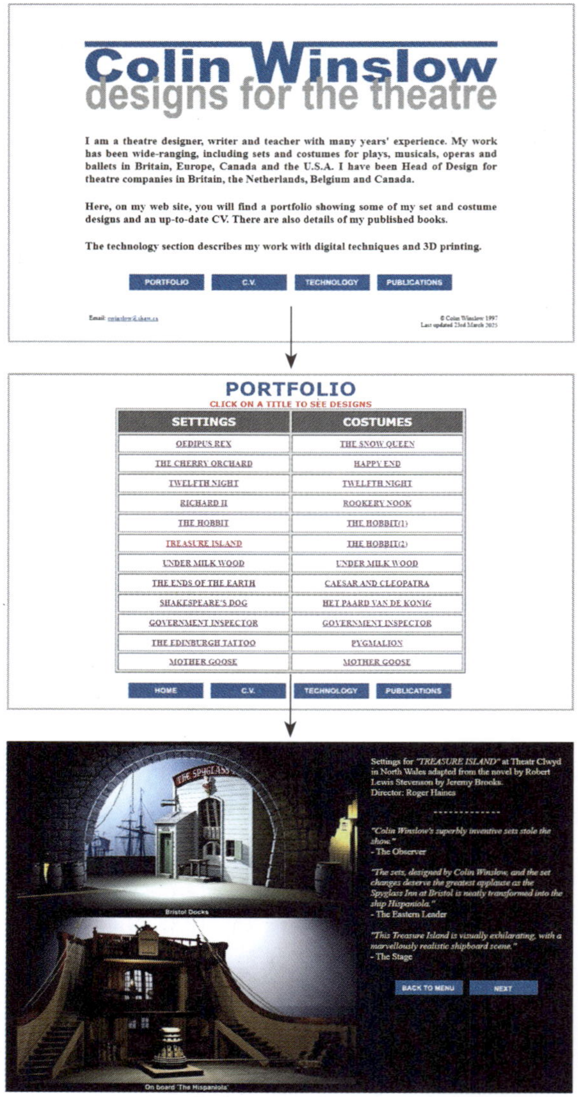

Navigating a website.

A favicon.

VIRTUAL REALITY

If you are lucky enough to have access to a 'viz room' your digital set model can be experienced in virtual reality. The room has walls formed by a continuous black back-projection screen, and a visitor wearing a stereoscopic visor and guided by a hand-held joystick can move around inside what appears to be the full-sized set. By this means, the director and actors can be given the opportunity to experience the completed set at an early stage in the rehearsal period.

If the digital model includes the whole theatre and not just the scenery, the actors can pass through doors, move behind the set, or look out towards the auditorium as they would during a performance. The effect can be disconcerting, as it is easy to drift through the digital walls and furniture, and often the exercise becomes somewhat self-defeating, as new participants find the experience itself so remarkable that they tend to forget that the purpose of the visit is to familiarise themselves with the set in which they are to perform.

The photograph below shows the cast and director of *Crimes of the Heart* on the first day of rehearsal, viewing the set in the viz room in the Department of Computing Science at the University of Alberta. Unfortunately, as a stereoscopic visor is needed for the full effect, a photograph can give only a very inadequate impression of the actual experience.

Viewing a set in virtual reality.

DIGITAL PEOPLE

A large part of a theatre designer's output is produced to scale, so designers and theatre technicians become very familiar with the standard scales, and will instantly be able to differentiate between a drawing at, say, scale 1:50 and one at scale 1:25. However, designers also have to communicate their ideas to people such as actors and directors, who may not be so technically proficient, so the inclusion of a human figure at the same scale can often be a help. Even for those used to working to scale, the figure will serve to keep the current scale constantly in mind. For the same reason, many designers like to keep a simple cut-out model of a human figure prominent on their work table when building set models.

With CAD, it is easy to include an outline drawing of a human figure at the same scale on sheets of technical drawings. In *AutoCAD* the figure can be drawn using a series of disconnected polylines converted to a single object with the 'GROUP' command. For designers lacking confidence in their drawing skills, a suitable digital photograph may be imported as a guide, and deleted when the traced outline is complete. The average male height in the UK is 1.78m, and the average female height is 1.62m. A male figure is generally used for purposes of scale, as being closer to 2m in height it makes comparisons a little easier, but a

CAD figures.

Cut-out scale figure in costume. .

female figure could also be used. The two figures opposite, which were created for the *Shakespeare's Dog* drawings, also give an indication of the type of costumes to be worn.

Having created a human figure to be added to technical drawings, it is easy to print a 1:25 version on to cardstock, then cut it out and glue a support at the back so that it can stand in the set model as a guide to scale. If costume designs are available, one of these may be scanned, reduced to scale and printed to card for use in the same way. Taking it a step further: with the use of bitmapped graphics software, the face on the costume design may be replaced with a photograph of the actual actor's face, to create a fairly realistic cut-out of the actor wearing the costume designed for the role. The photograph of the set model for *The Government Inspector* on page 73 contains a figure made in this way.

Fully modelled three-dimensional scale figures may also be included in set models. The figure in the photograph at right was modelled in *Poser* (see below), then, with the addition of a flat base to give a firm footing, it was printed to scale on a 3D printer.

3D-printed *Poser* figure.

Commercial 3D scanning booths are sometimes to be found in locations such as shopping malls and leisure centres, which can make a detailed full-body 3D scan of a human figure in just two or three minutes. The subject stands on a small, slowly revolving platform while a camera travels up the whole height of the figure, taking a large number of photographs as it moves. The photographs are then digitally combined to produce a 3D image of the entire figure. Shortly afterwards, the result can be viewed and revolved online, and full-colour 3D prints may be ordered in a variety of sizes. For theatre designers, this means that a realistic, fully coloured 3D print of a human figure may be included in set models. The photograph overleaf shows a 3D print of the author at scale 1:25 that was created in a scanning booth.

A full-body scanning booth is, of course, not intended for personal use, and unfortunately photogrammetry software such as *Meshroom* (see page 19) that works by combining photographs from a hand-held camera, is not generally very successful when scanning the entire body. However, the next photograph shows a 3D print of 'Alex', which was downloaded from *The Thingiverse* (https://www.thingiverse.com/

Figure printed from a full-body scan.

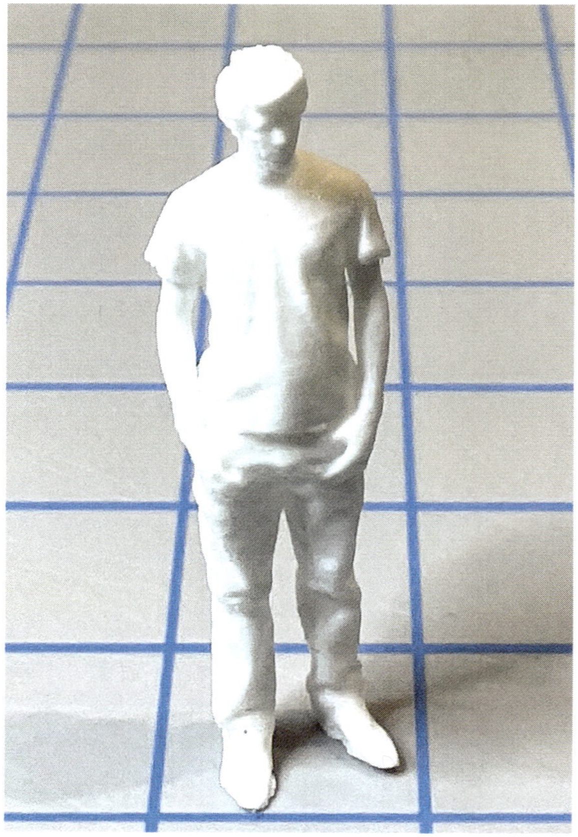

Printed figure from *The Thingiverse*.

thing:758728). It was created by Tim Howe from a full-body scan produced by the ingenious use of a Microsoft Xbox *Kinect* sensor and a home-made electrically powered turntable controlled by his own 3D-printed worm gear and spur cog. Sadly, not many of us have the technical skills needed for this kind of work, but at least we can download the results for our 3D printers. Other human figures are also available from *The Thingiverse* and similar websites.

Whenever a new piece of technology comes on to the market it is often prohibitively expensive and not particularly user-friendly, but as subsequent versions are developed, the price falls as the technology improves. So perhaps costume designers can look forward to the day when, at a costume fitting, a full-body scan of the actor wearing the still unfinished costume can be made in the fitting room. The costume could then be completed digitally, and an appropriate hairstyle and accessories added, so that a scaled 3D print of the fully costumed actor could be displayed in the set model, long before the completed costume becomes available.

POSER

(https://www.posersoftware.com)

Poser is a sizeable software package for creating, posing, clothing and rendering the human figure in 3D. It is particularly useful to theatre designers as the figures it creates can be exported for use in digital renderings or sent to a 3D printer for inclusion in a physical set model.

The program has seven 'rooms', named 'Pose', 'Material', 'Face', 'Hair', 'Cloth', 'Setup' and 'Content', which contain specialised controls for handling that specific aspect of the figure. On opening, the user is presented with the 'Pose' room, containing a stylised default figure, which can be replaced with one of the (improbably attractive) male or female stock figures included in the package, or with a figure purchased online

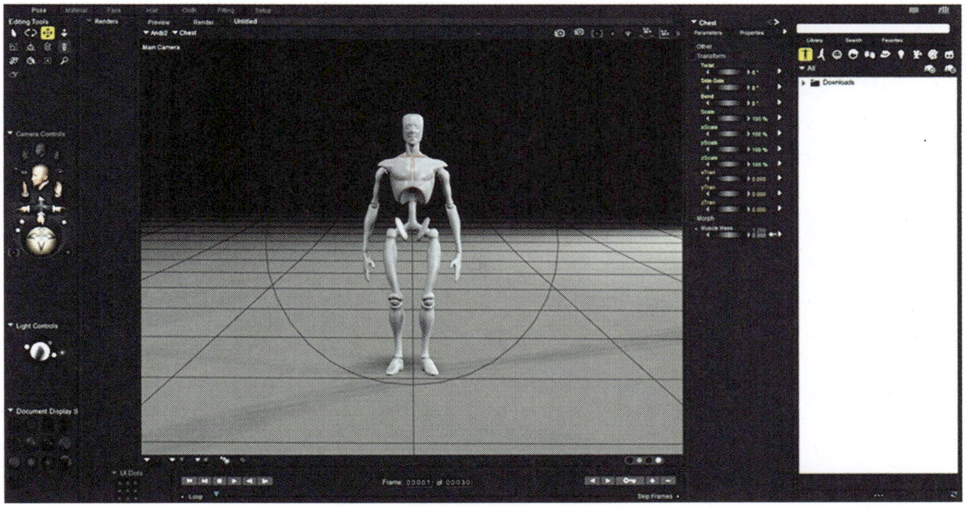

Initial *Poser* work screen with stylised human figure.

Poser figure imported into a digital set model.

from one of many independent developers. Included beside the work screen are a camera-control panel for changing the angle of view, a lighting-control panel, and a series of tools for adjusting the pose via an 'inverse kinetics' system (*see* the box on page 95).

The various 'rooms' offer a range of stock features that can be modified as desired, or developed entirely from scratch – although this is a much more complicated and time-consuming process. The huge range of available controls can be somewhat daunting at first, but with a little effort it is possible to create a realistic 3D digital figure with any type of body, and wearing individually designed clothing and hairstyle.

Costume designers may look forward to software that will automatically create perfect cutting diagrams, scaled to the performer's measurements, from a costume designed on a digitally generated figure – but in spite of spectacular developments in the use of AI, this particular feature is probably still a very long way off.

Poser face with dramatic lighting added.

Inverse Kinetics

Inverse kinetics is a mathematical process that helps to create natural-looking poses when a digital human figure is manipulated by the user. The figure is based on a skeleton of rigid parts that are linked together in a 'kinematic chain', which means that when one part is moved, the rest follow in a natural manner. For example: if a finger is moved a little away from the body, instead of being separated, the hand and arm will follow it – and if it is then moved further in the same direction, the body will bend to follow the arm, with the head and neck moving with the body, just as they would in real life.

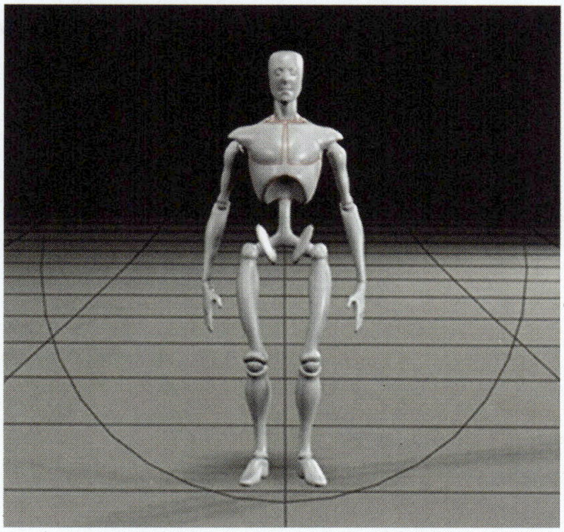

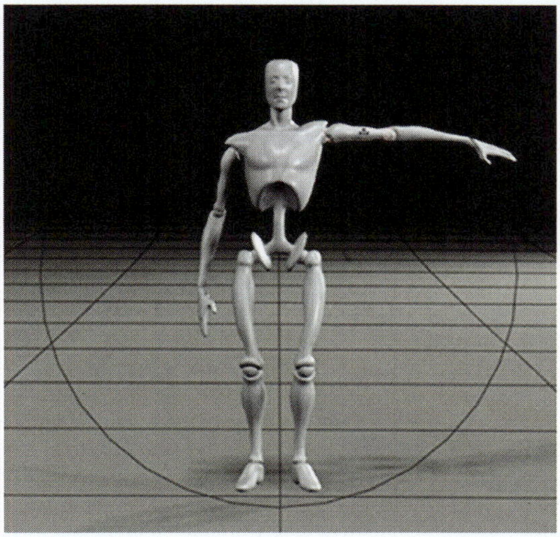

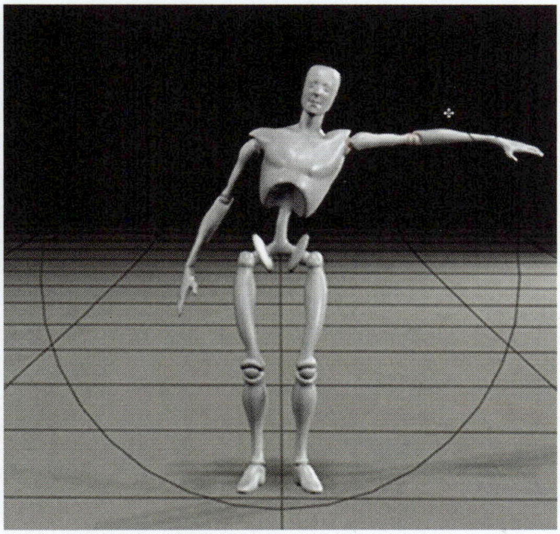

Inverse kinetics.

7
COSTUME DESIGNS

The set designer's main means of communication are technical drawings and scale models, the creation of which can be greatly assisted and enhanced by digital technology. A two-dimensional image is a welcome adjunct but is rarely considered a necessity, and now usually consists of a computer-generated image requiring little or no drawing skill. When designing costumes, however, some old-fashioned freehand drawing skills are still a great advantage, if not a necessity. There are various ways of getting round this requirement with the help of a computer – some of which are suggested below, but the results are generally less effective and usually take longer to produce than hand-rendered designs in pencil and watercolour, and this can be a serious drawback when a large number of costume designs are needed in a very short time.

The purpose of a costume design is to communicate the designer's concept to a group of people, who will each look at the design from a slightly different perspective: the director will want to know what the completed costume will look like and if it is appropriate for the production he has in mind; the actor will want to know what clothes he or she will be wearing on stage – especially in a fantasy or period play when the clothes will probably be very different from those worn in real life; the wardrobe supervisor will want to know the amount and type of fabrics required and if any special trimmings or other accessories will need to be ordered, and the cutter will look at the style in order to prepare cutting patterns; the lighting designer, on the other hand, will be primarily interested in the range of colours – and answers to all these questions are expected to be found in the costume designer's renderings.

If the designer has reasonably good freehand drawing skills, the design can also turn out to be an attractive and admired artwork, which has the extra advantage that the wardrobe department will probably work a little more enthusiastically and produce a slightly better costume; so the actor will be a little happier wearing it, and consequently give a better performance – and the end result will be that the costume designer will be considered

Computer-generated costume designs for *The Government Inspector.*

to be talented and will be offered more work. So even in this digital age, it is advantageous for costume designers to spend a little time and effort developing their freehand drawing skills.

Whatever method is used to produce them, hard-copy versions of costume designs are essential, particularly for costume makers, so when complete, they should be scanned and printed out in colour so that copies may be distributed to everyone involved in the production, and the original artwork can remain in the designer's portfolio without running the risk of being defaced by wear and tear or carelessly scribbled notes. An A3 page size is practical for the originals – this is a standard sketchbook size, and one that is large enough to be seen clearly during the design presentation; but they may need to be scanned and reduced to a smaller size later so that multiple copies can be made available for general circulation from a desktop printer.

The costume design at right is for a character in a production of the 1920s farce *Rookery Nook* at the Pitlochry Festival Theatre in Scotland. It was originally hand-drawn in pencil, with some details painted in watercolour, but leaving the patterned fabric areas blank. When a suitable fabric had been sourced, a piece of it was scanned and a repeat-area isolated. The costume design was also scanned, and the pencil lines intensified with bitmapped graphics software to create a more solid outline. The patterned areas were then digitally 'filled' with the scanned fabric design, considerably reduced in size. Finally, some simple Art Deco decoration was added around the sides of the sheet to emphasise the period – a significant design feature in this production.

Costume design for *Rookery Nook*.

BACK-UPS

When working on any lengthy computer-based project, you are strongly advised to save your work at frequent intervals as separate files under consecutively numbered file names. This may seem tedious when working under pressure, but it is a small chore when contrasted with the value of having access to a long sequence of earlier versions. Most programs permit a number of 'undos' that allow the user to step back through several changes made during a work session, and some programs, such as *AutoCAD*, automatically retain a back-up copy whenever work is re-saved – but these are not always helpful to designers, who sometimes need to revert to a version created much earlier: say, several days before.

When working on costume designs, it is particularly useful to be able to return to a version before any of the patterned or textured 'fills' have been added, because although a fully coloured and textured design gives a better overall impression of how the costume will appear on stage, many details, such as pleats and buttons, can be seen much more clearly in the outline rendering. Furthermore, as these types of detail are of particular interest to costume makers, a copy of the design at this earlier stage should be scanned and saved, to be passed to the wardrobe department to help when draughting cutting patterns or estimating costs.

While working on a production, it is a good idea to save all your work to a USB stick every day or two, so that if a serious disaster should occur – such as the ceiling collapsing on to your desk and destroying your computer, or the 'cloud' dispersing for some reason – it is still possible to retrieve most of the work you have already done.

Design before the addition of fabric pattern.

SPEEDING THINGS UP

The costume designs in the introductory illustration to this chapter are from a total of twenty-seven costumes designed for the production of *The Government Inspector* discussed earlier. These designs had to be very speedily produced as unfortunately the original costume designer had unexpectedly dropped out, and as the scheduled design deadline had already passed and the wardrobe department was eager to start work as soon as possible, speed was a major consideration.

Design work began, as usual, with some rapid pencil sketches, most of which were deliberately left incomplete. The sketches were then scanned and completed digitally in *Corel PHOTO-PAINT*, copying body parts such as arms, hands, legs and feet from side to side and from one sketch to another. The completed full-body sketches were then printed and refined by hand, solidifying the pencil lines, erasing any extraneous parts, and filling in gaps. For the sake of speed, facial features were either only lightly indicated with just a few dots and dashes, or omitted altogether. Repeating fill patterns, consisting mostly of stripes or checks, were created, and the re-digitised designs were completed by filling the fabric areas with these patterns or with solid colours. Finally, the designs were printed individually to hard copy, with names and a few notes added by hand.

The process of continually printing and scanning produced designs that were a more-or-less equal combination of both digital and manual drawing techniques, and as they contained many repeated elements, meant that the whole sequence could be created in a very short time.

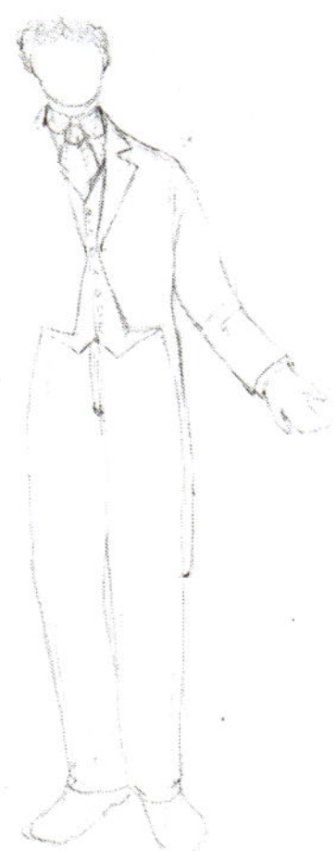

Original pencil sketch.

Sketch scanned and mirrored.

Digitally adjusted outline.

Colour and patterned fills added.

WHAT IF I CAN'T DRAW?

The immediate answer to this question is 'Learn!' for, with a little time and effort, anyone can acquire sufficient basic drawing skills to produce an effective costume design. The best way to learn to draw is to enrol in a regular life-drawing class at your local art school. Failing that, one of the many 'how-to' books on the subject, such as *Drawing the Head & Figure* by Jack Hamm, can be a helpful guide and a useful source of basic imagery.

There are many drawing courses available online, and although they are a poor substitute for in-person classes with a sympathetic teacher, they can prove helpful and are often free. However, note that some of them encourage the development of a type of caricature or a slick, anime style of imagery instead of really versatile drawing skills, and these should be avoided.

Bitmapped graphics programs such as *Photoshop* have wonderfully effective tools for manipulating and enhancing images, but they will not teach you how to draw. However, when combined with a printer/scanner, a pencil, and a few sheets of tracing paper – plus a little ingenuity – they can produce a reasonably effective imitation of a hand-drawn costume design with no real drawing skill involved.

Begin by creating some two-dimensional 'lay figures' similar to the small jointed three-dimensional figures that artists often use as an aid when drawing people. Find suitable frontal pictures of nude or semi-nude human figures online or in books. The female figure overleaf is from Jack Hamm's book on figure drawing, and the male figure on page 105 is from a photograph of an ancient Greek statue. Scan and/or save the selected images, trim the pages fairly close to the figure, and save them at a consistent resolution and size – say, 300 dpi and 297mm (A4) in height. The width will vary depending on the figure.

The pose may need to be adjusted in a bitmapped graphics program to provide a more appropriate basis for a costume design. In the female drawing overleaf, a face from another drawing has been substituted for the original one, and in both the male and female drawings bent arms have been straightened by copying the straight arm and mirroring it to the other side. Don't worry about any small inconsistences or inaccuracies at this stage – they can be ironed out later. Other small adjustments have also been made to avoid a completely symmetrical figure, by substituting parts from other images.

Print out the new image at the largest size your printer can conveniently handle, tape a sheet of tracing paper over it and quickly trace off the figure in pencil, omitting most of the interior details, and concentrating mainly on the pose's outline. Don't attempt total accuracy, but take some care over those parts that are generally considered difficult to draw, such as the hands, feet and face. Make several versions of the basic male and female figures, then scan and save them in a versatile format such as JPG or TIFF – all at the same resolution and height. You should now have a collection of basic two-dimensional male and female figures ready for use in various guises.

Reference image.

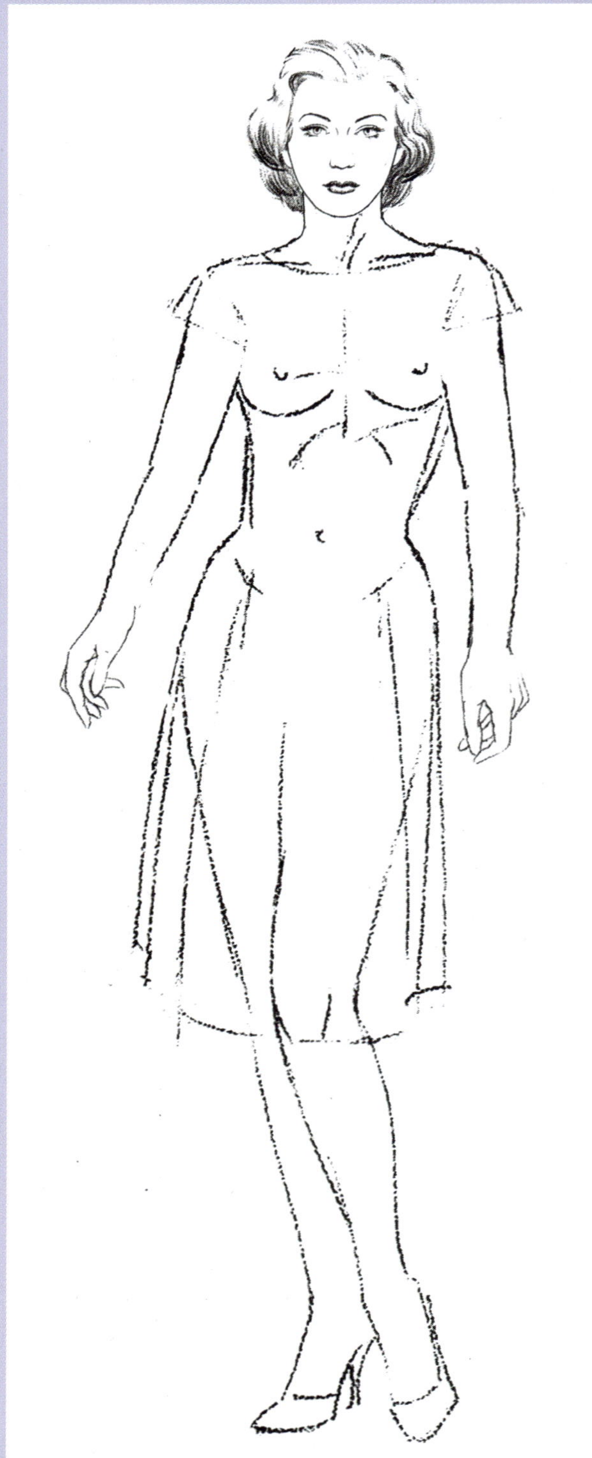

Reference image with digitally adjusted head, arm and hands.

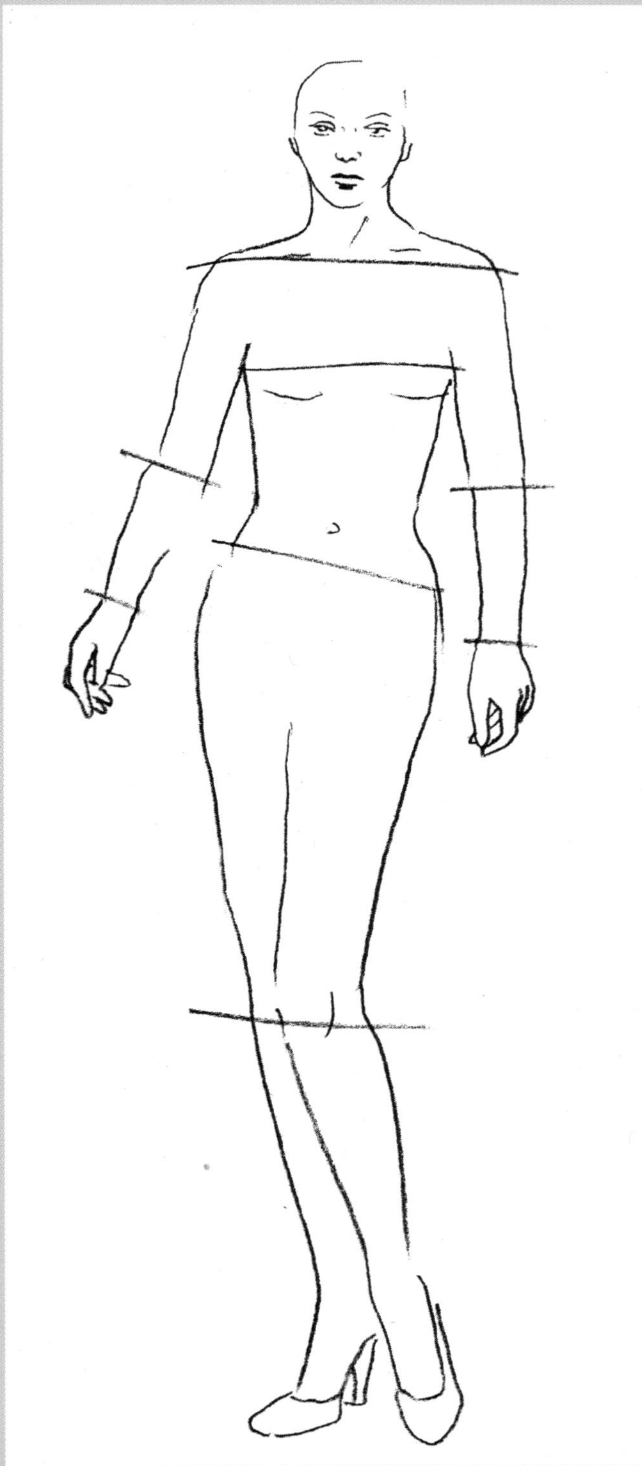

Traced version for use as a lay figure.

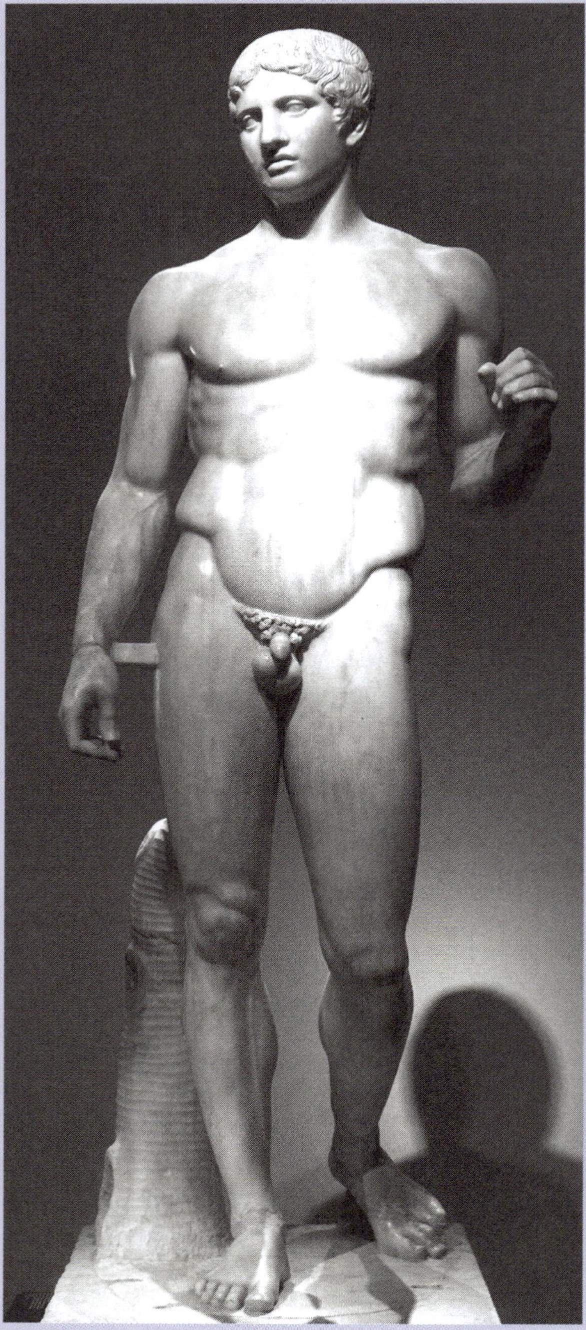

Reference picture.

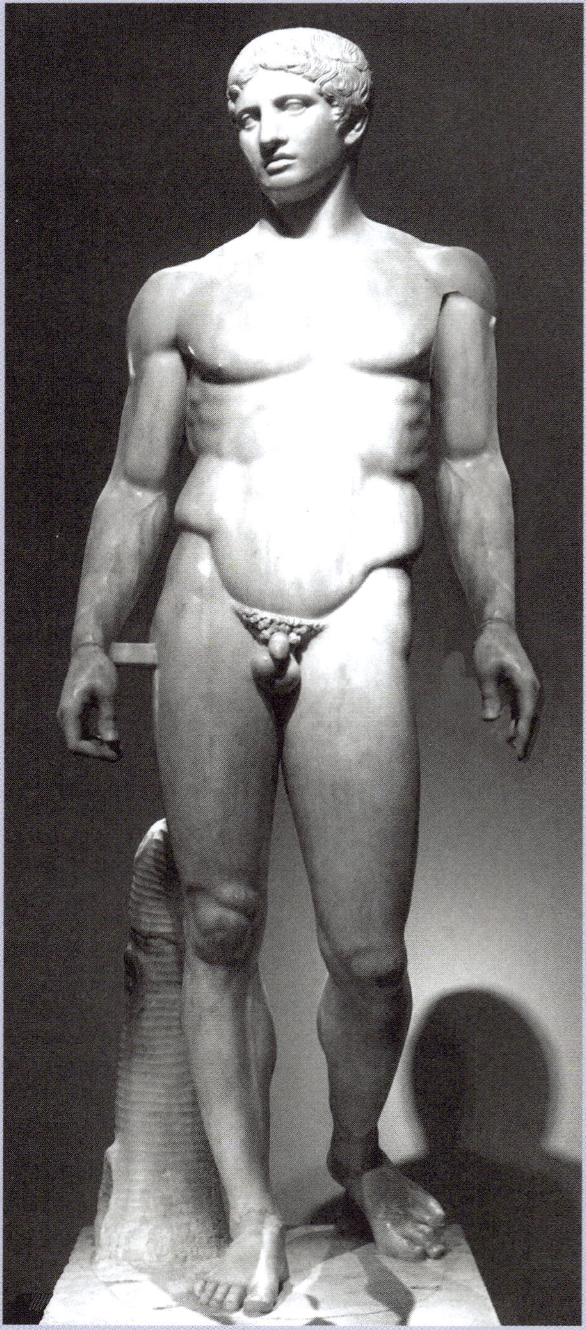

Reference image with digitally adjusted arm.

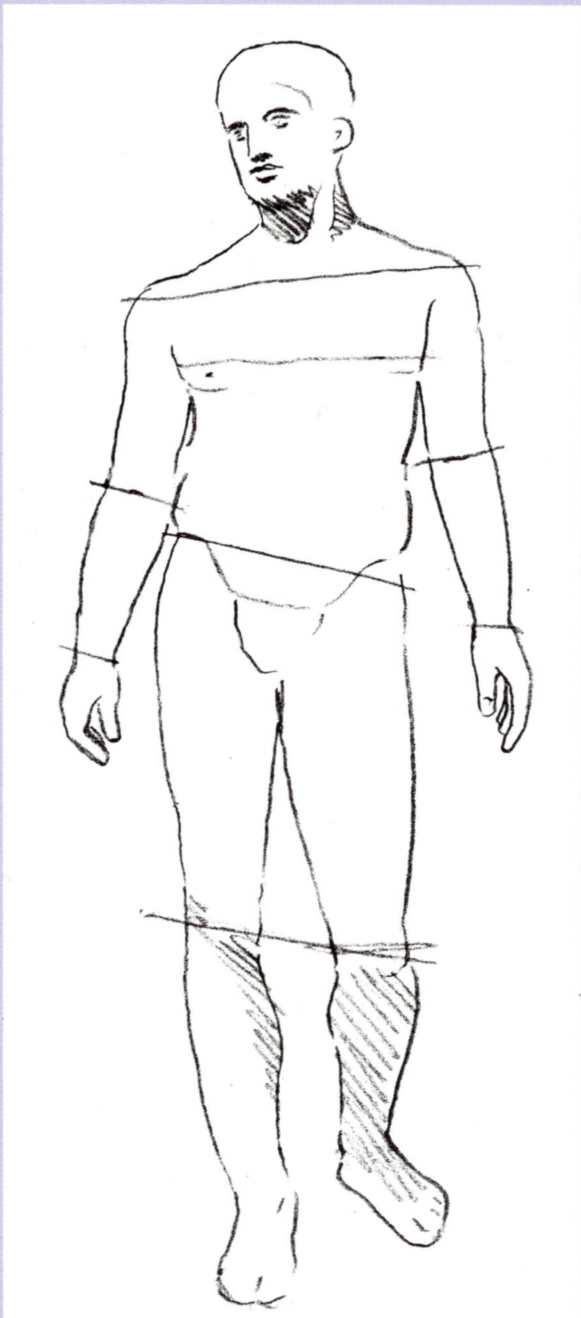

Traced version for use as a lay figure.

ADDING CLOTHING

Period costumes inevitably involve some research, but for designers less confident in their drawing skills, familiar contemporary clothing will also require a search for suitable reference material, either online or as pictures in books and magazines, to be used as a drawing guide. Look for individual elements that are appropriate for the costume you have in mind – details such as sleeves, collars, skirts, breeches, trousers, footwear, hairstyles and headgear can be selected from a variety of sources.

Outline-only images are needed here, so if the pictures are in the form of photographs, trace off the outlines with tracing paper and pencil, then scan and scale the tracings to approximately the same size at the lay figure images, and save them in the same format. If the costume detail images are already in a digital format, load them into your favourite bitmapped graphics software and select just those parts you wish to use, cutting out the irregular shapes using a freehand mask, and save them to file.

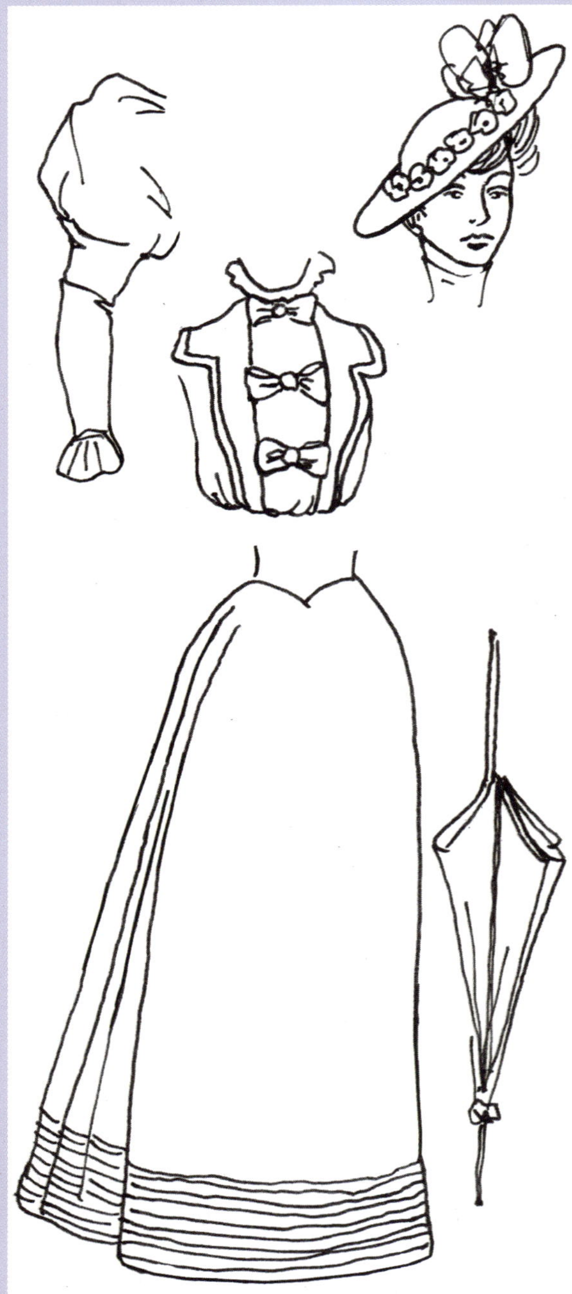

Costume details traced from reference material.

Costume details digitally superimposed on lay figure.

Final tracing.

Next, load one of your lay figures into the graphics program and begin the process of clothing it by importing each of the saved costume details individually and adjusting them to the figure by flipping, stretching and re-sizing to fit. Do not aim for a perfectly clean and accurate image at this stage – any unwanted elements can be eliminated and small gaps filled in later.

When the costume looks more or less complete, print it out at full-page size, and trace the outline of the entire figure again in pencil on tracing paper, omitting any extraneous lines and making small adjustments as required. Do not aim for a completely accurate finished image – a slightly 'sketchy' freehand style is preferable here. Scan the traced image, load it into the graphics program, adjust the outline colour to a darkish grey to simulate a pencil drawing, and save again. You should now have what appears to be a hand-drawn design ready for colouring.

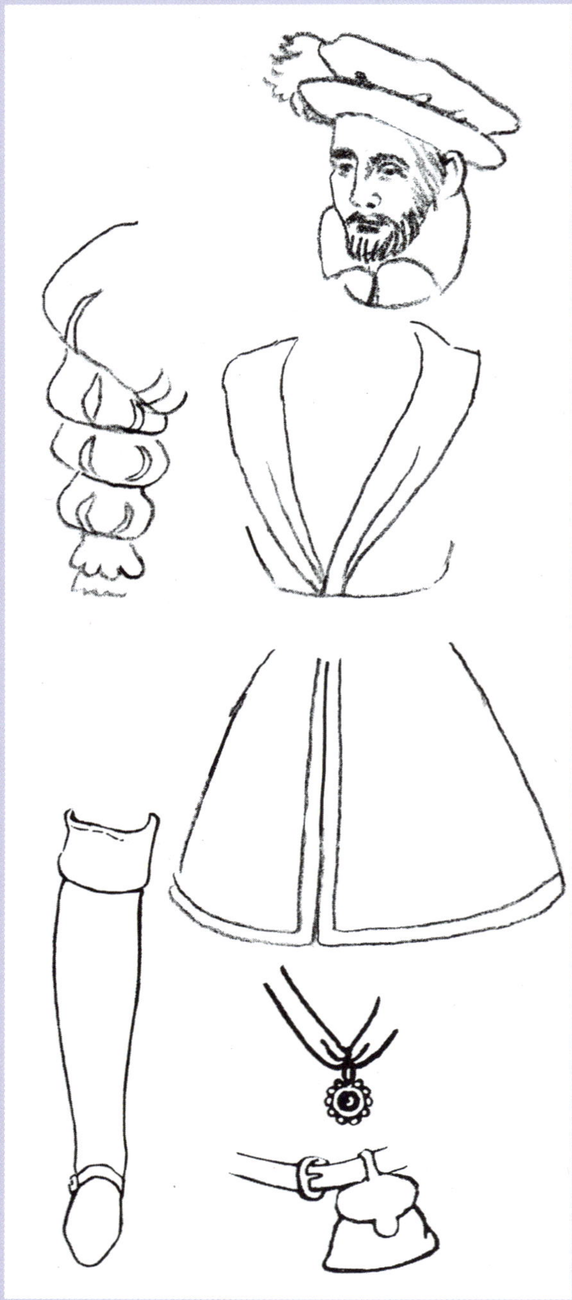

Costume details traced from reference material.

Costume details digitally superimposed on lay figure.

Final tracing.

APPLYING COLOUR

Colour may be added to the 'pencil sketch' either digitally or by hand. Colour applied by hand will best maintain the hand-rendered appearance, and requires only a minimum of artistic skill. First print two or three copies of each design on to printer cardstock – this is sturdier than paper and will prevent wrinkling and stretching when watercolour is applied. Mix the paints to the colours desired adding plenty of water so that it looks more like dye than paint, then apply these coloured washes to the costume drawing in swift broad strokes from a large brush.

This is not a 'colouring-book' style, so it is not necessary to keep precisely to the outlines. If you have printed out several copies of the outline drawing, you don't have to worry about making mistakes, as you can simply discard any unsatisfactory attempts and start again with a fresh sheet. Finer details such as trimmings and accessories can be picked out with a smaller brush and a little more care when the washes are dry.

If you choose to colour the designs digitally, a little preparation of the graphics software is required. Work on a copy of the stored design, so that if the 'pencilled' outline gets lost during the colouring process, it can be restored by copying just the outline from the original version with a colour mask set to accept just the outline colour, and 'pasting' it over the work in progress. Set up a fairly large-sized digital brush with about 85 per cent transparency and a wide soft or 'feathered' edge, then using the mouse, touch-screen or a graphics tablet, apply the colours rapidly in bold strokes, building up the colour intensity with repeated strokes to imitate the effect of transparent watercolour. Again, do not worry too much about keeping precisely to the outlines, but aim for a fairly casual style. Any major inaccuracies can be cleaned up later with the digital eraser.

To soften the plain white background, as in the male costume design below, first protect the figure with a colour mask so that only the white background is active, then apply a few rapid strokes in a pale neutral tone using a very large-sized digital brush and a high transparency level. The amount of background tone applied is a matter of personal preference, but the effect may be softened or otherwise adjusted after application by using the same digital brush set to white.

Finally, write the names of the actors and characters portrayed on a scrap of paper; scan them and copy them to the designs before saving them to the appropriate folder and printing them to hard copy for circulation.

Digitally coloured costume designs.

8

MORE ABOUT 3D PRINTING

On acquiring a 3D printer, theatre designers quickly discover the many ways it can help in their work – especially by shortening the length of time spent in building scale models. However, inventive users will want to experiment with some of its less generally appreciated possibilities, so the techniques described in this chapter are not directly related to the creation of set or costume designs – although some of them may be of interest to a theatre's wardrobe or props departments.

3D-printed interlocking links.

INTERLOCKED OBJECTS

3D printers can print several unconnected objects at the same time, skipping from one to another as each layer is laid down. This also works if the objects are interlocked, such as the four chain links in the illustration at right, designed by Stefan Langemark and downloaded from *The Thingiverse* (https://www.thingiverse.com/thing:28405). To create the long chain, links were arranged around the platen in a loose coil, carefully positioning each link so that it interlocked with its neighbour without actually touching it.

Using the same interlocking technique, special links can be designed that will interlock on all four sides to produce a flexible chainmail. Unfortunately,

3D-printed chain.

3D printing on to a fabric base.

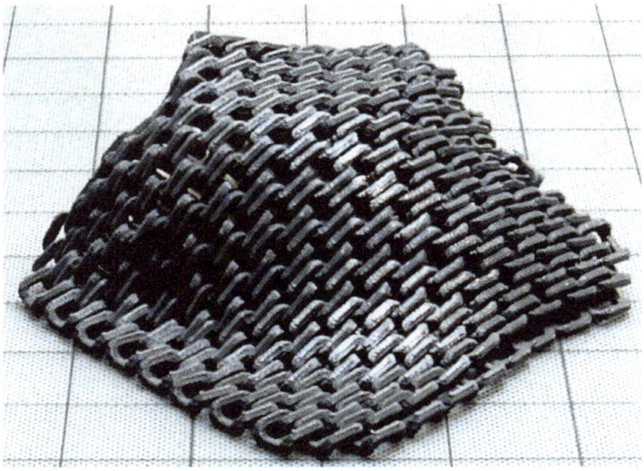

3D-printed chainmail.

its usefulness is severely limited by the size of the printer's platen. At the time of writing, the 3D printer with the biggest print size (142 × 111.6 × 153.6cm) is The *Massivit 10000* (https://www.massivit3d.com), which could produce pieces of chainmail of a wearable size but is a huge industrial machine, far beyond the resources of most theatres. Alternatively, special 'split-links' might be designed with a tiny break in them that could be used to link the pieces together. The 3D-printed piece of chainmail in the picture above measures 11.5cm square. It was designed by Trombo and is available for download from *The Thingiverse.* (https://www.thingiverse.com/thing:2942351)

A 3D-PRINTED ALPHABET

Constructing letters for 3D printing is not difficult, and a stored alphabet of extrudable letters can prove useful in many projects. First select a suitable font, and type out the entire alphabet in a bitmapped graphics program with a large point size and leaving a clear space between each letter. Use of the 'bold' print style will conveniently add a little extra thickness. Capital letters are most frequently needed, but lower case letters might also be included. Save the whole alphabet as a JPG image, then import it into a 3D modelling program. Enlarge the image, lock it into position, and carefully draw round the outline of each letter with a polyline, closing the line when complete to create an extrudable shape. The 'closed counters' or interior spaces that occur in the letters A, B, D, O, P, Q and R need to be outlined separately.

The imported JPG image can now be deleted, and each letter saved individually in DWG format. When you have a project that requires 3D lettering, copy the letters you need to the work screen, where they can be re-sized and extruded to the height required, subtracting the extruded interior shapes from those letters that contain them.

The three-dimensional letters can be used to create embossed inscriptions, either by applying them to the surface for raised lettering, or by setting them into the object and extracting them for incised letters. Personalised objects such as those in the photograph below can be created by arranging the appropriate extruded letters on to a base of some kind, combining all the parts into a single object with a 'UNION' command, and exporting the result to STL format for printing.

3D-printed name plates and key-ring tag.

CHANGING COLOURS DURING PRINTING

Some 3D printers, such the Bambu Lab range (*see* page 67) are designed as multicolour printers, holding several spools of coloured filament at the same time and switching between them as pre-programmed with the printer's preparation software. This facility can produce some very attractive results, but has little practical use for set designers, who need access to an infinitely wide range of colours with carefully textured and gradated effects of a kind that are best produced with paint and a brush.

Most filament-based 3D printers have the ability to pause the printing process at any time, and resume printing later from exactly the same point. This makes it possible to change the reel of filament while the printer is paused, then continue printing with a different coloured filament. The decorative plaque in the picture below demonstrates this technique: when the red base layers had been laid down, printing was paused, the filament was changed to white for the lettering, then printing continued. Unfortunately, unless the printer's software allows the 'pause' point to be predetermined, this method can be time-consuming, as the user has to keep a watchful eye on the progress of the print, to pause and change the filament at just the right time.

3D-printed plaque in two colours.

3D PRINTING ON TO FABRICS

Using the 'pause print' technique, after the first few layers, instead of changing the filament during the pause, a piece of gauze or some other thin, loosely woven fabric may be placed over the print and temporarily fixed to the platen with adhesive tape around its edges. Then, when printing is resumed, the result is a piece of fabric with the 3D-printed object or objects not merely applied to its surface, but firmly set into it. In the example overleaf, two decorative capital letters were extruded to a height of less than a millimetre, and printing was paused after the first three layers so that a piece of fine gauze could be placed over them and printing continued until complete.

Using this technique, a piece of fabric can be produced with an embedded arrangement of three-dimensional objects by first creating the objects in a 3D modelling program, positioning a group of them into a grid formation, and saving the whole array as a single file. The objects may be flat, with just a small amount of thickness, or truly three-dimensional as seen in the illustration at the head of this chapter. Flexible spiked or 'scaly' fabrics can also be created in this way, with elongated or curved interlocking spikes embossed (see illustrations on the following page). As with the chainmail example referred to earlier, practical applications of this technique are limited by the size of the printer's platen, but items such as studded collars or spiked wrist-straps for fantasy costumes can easily be created on a desktop 3D printer.

3D-printed letters set into gauze.

3D-printed scales on fabric.

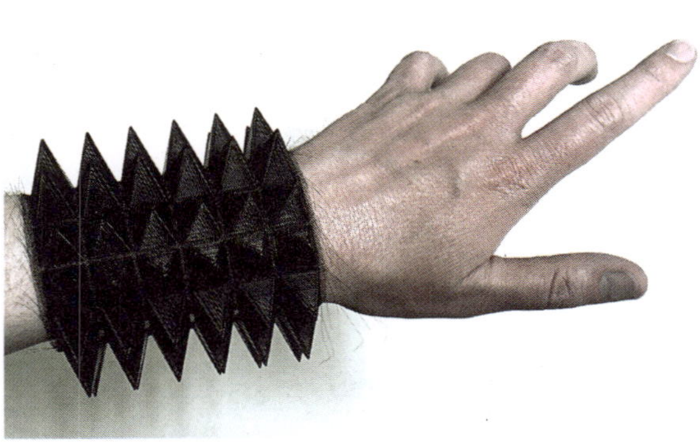

3D-printed spiked wrist-strap.

3D-PRINTED OBJECTS FOR THE WORK TABLE

Theatre designers will discover many objects that are easy to design and quick to produce on a 3D printer, which can be useful in their work space. The picture opposite shows a few of such items.

Left: Two 'wash cups' to hold watercolour washes when painting costume designs or set models. The cups have rounded bottoms inside for easy cleaning, and indentations around the rim to hold the paintbrush when not in use.

Centre: A shallow dish to hold glue when model-making. Cocktail sticks or toothpicks are the best tools for applying a small amount of glue in just the right place, and the small holes round the side of the dish will hold several of them ready for use.

Top right: A container for spare cocktail sticks – just the right height, so their tops are free to be easily grabbed when they are needed.

Bottom right: A small block to be used as a three-dimensional set square when gluing pieces of cardboard at right angles to each other. Running the block along the join between pieces that have just been placed into position will not only correct the angle, but also remove any excess adhesive. (*See* inset picture.)

3D PRINTING IN OTHER MATERIALS

Filaments designed to imitate materials such as metal, stone or wood are available for desktop 3D printers – some are more effective than others, but commercial 3D printing services use specialised techniques to offer output in a wide range of materials including gold, silver, brass, copper, aluminium, stone and wood. The most popular technique, known as 'laser sintering', fuses together very fine particles of the actual material using a high-temperature laser beam.

Some useful items from a 3D printer.

The illustration shows a brass sealing-wax stamp produced by this method.

The most effective (and the most elaborate) method for producing high-quality metal objects is referred to as '3D printing and lost wax casting' because it is very similar to the traditional *cire perdue* foundry technique. Here the model is first printed using a wax-like resin, which is then covered in plaster and allowed to set, leaving a thin 'escape route' for molten wax. The plaster mould is then heated in an oven until all the wax has melted and drained away, creating a cavity of the same shape as the original model in the solid plaster. Next, molten metal such as bronze or silver is poured into the mould, filling the cavity, and left to cool and solidify. Finally, the plaster mould is broken apart to remove the solid metal object, which can be polished to whatever finish is required. It is a time-consuming and expensive technique, but one that would be appropriate for creating a one-off special object such as an award trophy.

3D-printed sealing-wax stamp in brass.

BIBLIOGRAPHY

CAD

Abbott, Dan *AutoCAD Secrets Every User Should Know* (Wiley Publishing Inc., 2007).
Useful information for those already familiar with the basic techniques.

Briedforda, Nuemiar *The Ultimate Autodesk 3ds Max 2025 Guide for Beginners* (Independently published, 2024).
Covers everything from installation to the most advanced techniques. Includes step-by-step instructions and many practical examples.

Brito, Allan *Blender 3D: Architecture, Buildings, and Scenery* (Packt Publishing Ltd, 2008).
Step-by-step tutorials using *Blender* to create realistic visualisations of building exteriors and interiors, including furniture and dressings. Of particular interest to set designers.

Chopra, Aidan *Google Sketchup for Dummies* (Wiley Publishing Inc.).
An introduction to this easy-to-use draughting and 3D modelling software in non-technical language. Updated editions are published as new versions of the software are introduced.

Cooper, Gavin and White, Christine *Computer Visualisation for the Theatre* (Focal Press, 2003).
Creative ideas and practical advice aimed specifically at set designers, including many sample projects.

Grabowski, Ralph *AutoCAD for Dummies* (Wiley Publishing Inc., 2022).
Step-by-step tutorials from the basics to advanced 3D techniques in non-technical language.

van Gumster, Jason *Blender for Dummies* (Wiley Publishing Inc.).
A good introduction to this free but complex 3D modelling software in non-technical language. Updated editions are published as new versions of the software are introduced.

Macluskie, Steve *Vectorworks for Theatre* (Entertainment Technology Press Ltd, 2015).
An easy-to-follow reference manual written by an experienced theatre technician and teacher, illustrated with many useful screen captures.

Ripley, David *AutoCAD – A Handbook for Theatre Users* (Entertainment Technology Press Ltd).
Written by an experienced theatre technician and teacher, and aimed specifically at theatre designers. Contains a series of theatre-based graded tutorials from the basics to 3D modelling. Frequently updated, so make sure you buy the most recent edition.

DRAWING

Aristides, Juliette *Lessons in Classical Drawing* (Watson-Guptill, 2011).

An excellent introduction to drawing techniques. Also contains a masterclass on DVD.

Hamm, Jack *Drawing the Head & Figure* (The Penguin Group (USA) Inc., 1983).

Simple but effective techniques for hand-rendering the human figure. A useful source of basic images to be developed into costume designs using graphics software.

Petroski, Henry *The Pencil – a History of Design and Circumstance* (Knopf, 1990).

An informative and entertaining book covering not only the invention and development of the graphite pencil, but also its influence in design, craftsmanship and manufacturing.

3D PRINTING

McMills, Anne E. *3D Printing Basics for Entertainment Design* (Routledge, 2018).

A comprehensive and profusely illustrated overview by a theatre lighting designer and teacher.

Prettis, Bre, Kaziunas France, Anna, and Shergill, Jay *Getting Started with MakerBot* (O'Reilly Media Inc., 2013).

A useful handbook for new owners of *MakerBot* 3D printers, covering a wide range of related topics.

THEATRE DESIGN

Winslow, Colin *The Handbook of Model Making for Set Designers* (The Crowood Press Ltd, 2008).

Winslow, Colin *The Handbook of Set Design* (The Crowood Press Ltd, 2006).

Winslow, Colin *The Handbook of Techniques for Theatre Designers* (The Crowood Press Ltd, 2010).

WEBSITE DESIGN

Flanders, Vincent, and Willis, Michael *Web Pages That Suck* (Sybex Inc. 1998).

A chatty but somewhat controversial classic that aims to encourage good website design by examining examples of bad design. Profusely illustrated, with supporting CD.

McClelland, Deke, Eismann, Katrin and Stone, Terri *Web Design Studio Secrets, 2nd Edition* (IDG Books Worldwide Inc., 2000).

Still an excellent guide for those wishing to get into the basics of web design. Profusely illustrated, with supporting CD.

Melch, Young *Essential Guide to Adobe Dreamweaver for All Levels* (Computer Guru Institute, 2023).

A comprehensive guide to using *Dreamweaver* software for the creation of websites. Particularly useful for beginners.

USEFUL WEBSITES

INSTRUCTION

https://www.aristidesarts.com/aristides-atelier

Website of Seattle-based artist/teacher Juliette Aristides, with examples of her work and links to her online drawing workshops and courses.

https://cad4theatre.org.uk

Site run by David Ripley, author of *AutoCAD – A Handbook for Theatre Users* (*see* Bibliography) containing a huge amount of *AutoCAD* information, including details of online courses aimed specifically at theatre users.

https://www.kaciehultgren.com

Website of Kacie Hultgren, 3D printing crusader, set designer and educator, with links to online tutorials.

ORGANISATIONS

https://www.abtt.org.uk

Association of British Theatre Technicians (ABTT): A professional organisation covering all fields of theatre technology, offering training courses, advice and safety information.

https://designers.ca

Associated Designers of Canada (ADC): Canadian equivalent of the SBTD, offering professional development opportunities and training courses in live performance design.

https://www.thealpd.org.uk

The Association for Lighting Production and Design (ALPD): An organisation representing all those who work in, or are interested in the creation of lighting for live performances and events across the full range of performance lighting disciplines in the UK.

https://www.citt.org

Canadian Institute for Theatre Technology (CITT): Canadian equivalent of the ABTT.

https://www.equity.org.uk

Equity: The trades union representing professional performers and creative workers of all kinds in the entertainment industries, including designers.

https://iatse.net

International Alliance of Theatrical Stage Employees (IATSE): Union of behind-the-scenes entertainment workers in the USA and Canada.

https://oistat.org

International Organisation of Scenographers Theatre Architects and Technicians (OISTAT): A global network of theatre makers celebrating design and technology in live performance. The site contains details of the *Prague Quadrennial*, a competitive exhibition of international performance design held every four years in Prague.

https://www.theatredesign.org.uk

Society of British Theatre Designers (SBTD): Details of forthcoming events and a list of members with contact details and pictures of their work.

https://www.usitt.org

United States Institute for Theatre Technology (USITT): The American equivalent of the ABTT.

PUBLICATIONS

https://all3dp.com

All3DP is an international online magazine for anyone interested in 3D printing at any level.

https://www.crowood.com

The Crowood Press Ltd: Publishers of this book and many others on aspects of technical theatre.

https://www.pantone.com

Pantone Matching System: A proprietary numbering system used worldwide for the accurate designation of colours.

https://www.thestage.co.uk

Online version of *The Stage*: The long-established weekly newspaper of the theatrical profession. Includes show reviews, 'Backstage and Technical' and 'Jobs' sections.

REFERENCE

https://artquest.org.uk

Artquest is a free resource offering advice, opportunities and information for artists and craftspeople. The *Artlaw* section gives legal advice and includes a useful 'Frequently Asked Questions' page with expert legal answers.

https://cad4theatre.org.uk/images/document/14851818/ABTTCADStandardsv2.1.pdf

The ABTT recommended CAD draughting standards for venue and production drawings.

https://www.siue/COSTUMES/history

Site of the Southern Illinois University Edwardsville containing a complete online version of the celebrated nineteenth-century costume reference plates *History of Costume* or *Zur Geschichte der Kostüme* by Braun and Schneider.

https://www.uktw.co.uk

UK Theatre Web containing much useful information about what's happening on the British theatre scene.

https:www.wga.hu

The Web Gallery of Art, containing thousands of high-resolution digital reproductions of European paintings and sculptures from the third to the nineteenth centuries, many with commentaries and biographies, also some 'guided tours'.

https://www.winslow.uk.com

The author's personal website.

SOFTWARE

https://www.adobe.com/acrobat/online/convert-pdf.html

A free program that will accept text or graphic files in any format and convert them to PDF.

https://www.adobe.com/uk/products/photoshop-elements.html

Photoshop Elements: Home of the most popular graphics program worldwide, enhanced with AI.

https://www.autodesk.com/products/autocad

Download page for *AutoCAD* – the theatre industry's standard draughting and 3D modelling software.

https://www.autodesk.com/products/3ds-max

3D Max: modelling, animation and CGI program from the same developer as *AutoCAD.* Particularly popular with games developers.

https://www.blender.org

Entirely free download and support for *Blender* 3D modelling and animation software.

https://www.bricsys.com/bricscad

BricsCAD CAD and 3D modelling software aimed at designers and engineers.

https://www.coreldraw.com

CorelDRAW Graphics Suite: An interrelated group of graphics programs that includes both vector graphics and bitmapped graphics.

https://affinity.serif.com/en-gb

Affinity Designer, Affinity Photo and *Affinity Illustrator*: interrelated programs for vector graphics, bitmapped graphics and graphical page layouts.

https://www.adobe.com/uk/products/dreamweaver.html

Dreamweaver software developed by Adobe for the creation of websites.

https://www.danstools.com

Dan's Tools: A sizeable collection of entirely free online tools for developing and checking websites.

https://www.favicon-generator.org

Free, easy-to-use tools for creating 'favicons' for websites, with details of how to use them. Included in *Dan's Tools* (above).

https://www.freecad.org

FreeCAD: Free, open-source CAD and 3D modelling software.

https://www.godaddy.com

GoDaddy: One of the biggest and most popular web-hosting sites, offering domain name registration, website building tools, marketing advice and more.

https://htmlcolorcodes.com

A free and easy-to-use colour-picker system for finding HTML codes for use in website design.

https://meshroom.en.softonic.com

Meshroom: Freely downloadable, open-source software for converting photographs to three-dimensional digital objects.

https://www.posersoftware.com

Poser: A software package distributed by Bondware for the creation, manipulation, animation and rendering of realistic 3D human figures.

https://www.progesoft.com

ProgeCAD from Progesoft: A less expensive alternative to *AutoCAD* with an almost identical interface.

https://www.rhino3d.com

Rhino 3D modelling software: Particularly useful for creating irregular or organic subjects.

https://www.sketchup.com

SketchUp: Low-priced, easy-to-use draughting and 3D modelling software.

https://imsidesign.com/products/turbocad

TurboCAD draughting and 3D modelling software available in several versions.

https://www.vectorworks.net

Site of *Vectorworks Spotlight*: Draughting and 3D modelling software aimed at theatre users. A popular alternative to *AutoCAD*.

https://cast-soft.com/wysiwyg-lighting-design

WYSIWYG design and visualisation software for performance lighting designers.

https://www.zoom.com

Home site of *Zoom* online conferencing systems.

SUPPLIERS

https://cricut.com/en-gb

Site of the *Cricut* range of smart cutters.

https://modelshop.co.uk

The *4D Model Shop* located under the arches in Leman Street, London, stocks practically everything you could possibly need for making set models; also available for purchase online.

https://www.plastruct.com

Plastruct Inc., based in Illinois USA, international suppliers of plastic parts for scale models of all kinds, available for purchase online. Catalogue downloadable in PDF format or available as hard copy for purchase.

https://emea.rosco.com

Rosco: International suppliers of products such as stage lighting equipment, including gels and gobos, smoke/fog machines, scene paints and much more.

https://www.silhouetteamerica.com

Site of the *Silhouette* range of smart cutters.

https://www.techsoft.co.uk

Based in Denbighshire since the mid-1980s, *TechSoft UK* is the leading supplier of all kinds of CAD/CAM equipment and software to educational establishments throughout the UK.

https://www.whitelight.ltd.uk

White Light Ltd: Stage lighting specialists since 1971, with offices in Wimbledon and Manchester, supplying equipment for sale or hire.

3D PRINTING

https://www.bambulab.com

Site of the *Bambu Lab* range of 3D printers.

https://bambulab.com/en/download/studio

Bambu Studio: contains free software for slicing and colouring *Bambu Lab* 3D prints.

https://www.creality.com

Site of the *Creality* range of 3D printers, laser engravers, 3D scanners etc.

https://www.elegoo.com

Site of the *Elegoo* range of FDM and resin-based 3D printers.

https://www.massivit3d.com

Site of *Massivit* industrial large-format 3D printers.

https://i.materialise.com

An easy-to-use, online 3D printing service headquartered in Belgium but offering an international service.

https://www.makerbot.com

Site of *MakerBot* 3D printers.

https://ministage.shop

Based in central London, *MiniStage* offers 3D printing for set models at 1:25 and 1:50 scales, either as specially created custom prints, or directly from their collection of furniture and other regularly used items. They also have a range of model-making supplies for sale.

https://www.prusa3D.com

Site of *Prusa* 3D printers.

https://www.thingiverse.com

Thingiverse: A site for sharing user-created object files for 3D printing. Literally thousands of designs are available for free download, some of which are particularly useful to theatre designers.

https://ultimaker.com/software/ultimaker-cura

UltiMaker Cura: free, easy-to-use 3D printing software, including a popular slicing engine.

https://www.chitubox.com/en/download/chitubox-free

Chitubox Basic: free, easy-to-use 3D printing software for resin-based printers.

INDEX

First published in 2026 by
The Crowood Press Ltd
Ramsbury, Marlborough
Wiltshire SN8 2HR

enquiries@crowood.com
www.crowood.com

British Library Cataloguing-in-Publication Data
A catalogue record for this book is available from the British Library.

For product safety-related questions, contact:
productsafety@crowood.com

ISBN 978 0 7198 4651 9

Typeset by Envisage IT

Cover design by Susan Richards

Printed and bound in India by Thomson Press India

Dedication
For Robin

Acknowledgements
Shane Marsh for photographs on pages 4, 66 and 67 and for printing the model on page 64. Also for advice on 3D printers and general technical information.

Ellis Bros. for the photograph on page 45.

Jaylon Grenier and Ken Matthews for allowing their 3D printers to be photographed.

Steven Barlott - hand model for the photograph on page 116.